T0350826

Copyright ©2004 by Charles C. Poirier, Lynette Ferrara, Francis Hayden, and Douglas Neal
ISBN 1-932159-08-8

Printed and bound in the U.S.A. Printed on acid-free paper
10 9 8 7 6 5 4 3 2 1

Library of Congress Cataloging-in-Publication Data

The networked supply chain : applying breakthrough business process management technology to meet relentless customer demands / by Charles C. Poirier ... [et al.].
    p. cm.
  ISBN 1-932159-08-8 (alk. paper)
  1. Business logistics.   2. Business networks.   I. Poirier, Charles C., 1936–
   HD38.5.N476 2003
   658.5—dc21

                                        2003009173

Phone: (561) 869-3900
Fax: (561) 892-0700
Web: www.jrosspub.com

The Networked Supply Chain

Applying Breakthrough BPM Technology to Meet Relentless Customer Demands

CHARLES POIRIER
LYNETTE FERRARA
FRANCIS HAYDEN
DOUGLAS NEAL

J.ROSS
PUBLISHING

APICS.
THE EDUCATIONAL SOCIETY
FOR RESOURCE MANAGEMENT

DEDICATION

For Bill Houser,
whose friendship and help never failed
Chuck Poirier

For Mike Bauer and Steve Reiter,
who, along with Chuck Poirier, introduced me to
the key ideas of advanced supply chain thinking
and have continued to be a source of inspiration
Lynette Ferrara

To Keren and all our fabulous children.
Pride can't really be a sin, can it?
Francis Hayden

For Sue, Kristen, and Justin —
You are my joy and sustenance.
Douglas Neal

CONTENTS

PREFACE

Supply chain management (SCM) has become a business manager's dream and a business manager's nightmare. Virtually every company in every industry all over the world puts SCM high up on its improvement agenda, as leaders believe they can make substantial gains by redesigning the supply chain process. For more than a decade, however, there has been a yawning gap between the rhetoric and the track record of most practitioners. There have been some successes — enough to keep the dream alive, but in most cases there has been little payback for all the time and money invested, and the entire effort is now stalled for many businesses.

Research into the results of supply chain programs shows a wide range of achievement, a sort of bell-shaped curve. The few companies at the top end are now a year or more ahead of their industry competitors and have added three to eight points of new profit to their bottom lines. Wal-Mart stands out as an example of a retail firm that has added several points of additional profit on revenues directly through its supply chain effort. The majority of companies, in the middle of the curve, have seen some measure of improvement for their labors, but are still struggling to gain more from the effort — especially on the outside, in the space between businesses where they have to collaborate. At the bottom end, organizations are finding it hard to realize any benefit at all. Companies in industries such as construction, forest products, and publishing tend to fall into this category. This difference in results presents a real opportunity for the winners and a real threat to the losers. If you can get ahead of the competition, there are significant extra profits to be made. If you fall behind, it could mean business failure.

The logic supporting supply chain efforts is compelling. By combining existing continuous improvement efforts with more ambitious projects to enhance the whole end-to-end process of acquiring materials or services, converting them into saleable goods and services, and delivering them to customers, you can save costs, improve performance, increase revenue, make better use of assets, and satisfy the unrelenting demands of your customers and the end consumers.

But that is easier said than done. Introducing useful internal changes is easy enough, but to get the real benefits you must enlarge the number of firms participating in the effort and collaborate with them to establish optimized network conditions for the whole chain — and that's where the problems start. The first problem that became apparent was a cultural inhibition that limited internal and external collaboration with supply chain partners. This problem is undoubtedly real, and in fact some sources blame everything on people's reluctance to abandon old ways of working, to trust their partner companies, and generally to think outside of the box. In our view, this is not the whole picture.

There is a second problem, which has more to do with practical realities. Technology struggles to support the higher levels of the supply chain optimization effort, existing technologies cannot keep pace with business demands, and they fail to deliver on the promises. Systems integration also costs too much, takes too long, and is not flexible enough to meet the emerging demands of most marketplaces. And even if the integration is successful, it does not provide the visibility, control, and coordination required to advance beyond the early, internal levels of a supply chain progression.

The few success stories, such as those coming from Adaptec, Boeing, Cisco, Dell, Intel, Procter & Gamble, Toyota, and Wal-Mart, are impressive, but they are exceptions. The majority of technology projects, including enterprise resource planning (ERP), supplier relationship management (SRM), customer relationship management (CRM), collaborative planning, forecasting, and replenishment (CPFR), and e-business, took too long, cost far more than projected, and failed to deliver the business results they set out to achieve. Indeed, the installation of ERP, which was heralded as the ultimate business solution, often did nothing at all to solve the intra- or interenterprise issues that inhibit supply chain collaboration.

The technical issues resulted from disparate infrastructures, systems that needed to be integrated without a uniform standard for doing so, and processes that crossed department and business boundaries, although there was no common language for working together even if the systems were connected. What was needed was the ability to plan and execute a process from end to end across several businesses, dozens of information technology (IT) systems, and many human agents, to customize it so that it could be unique to each customer segment or even each customer, and then to maintain visibility and control of each instance right across the enterprise. No technology so far has come anywhere near providing that capability, so, not surprisingly, few supply chain projects overcome the technical hurdle.

When projects get stalled, the symptoms are very evident. Customers complain they get lost in the network; they never know who to contact, how to check on an order, or how to discuss a new idea, particularly when more than one firm is involved in the support of a product or service. If the company insists on squeezing out costs even when the technology has not delivered the improved capability, the increasingly angry customers suffer what Shoshana Zuboff and James Maxmin have called the "little murders" — like the outsourced call center that infuriates rather than helps, the proliferation of products that no one wants, and the myriad new fees for services that were once seen as part of the basic product.* Meanwhile, suppliers and other partners complain that they need expensive new technology for every network in which they participate and that these networks rarely provide them the information they require to plan production. Many feel exasperated by the lack of any way to contribute their knowledge and expertise where they would really add value, in spite of constant assurances that such help is wanted and valued.

Business Process Management Technologies Are Designed to Solve These Problems

Business process management (BPM) technologies will provide every business, large or small, with an opportunity to participate in, or to lead, a supply chain effort and through it to become a viable part of a networked enterprise. With BPM, processes can be planned and deployed across people, systems, and business boundaries. The time and cost of deploying them are reduced because components of existing IT systems can be accessed and coordinated through the kind of standard interfaces

---

* Shoshana Zuboff and James Maxmin, *The Support Economy*, Viking, 2002.

that are rapidly replacing older, hard-wired integration technologies. New data integration and modeling tools speed the development of common trading languages within businesses or supply networks. With BPM, managers and IT staff can work together to build business process models that they all understand, that can be simulated and tested, and which actually drive the execution of the process from end to end. The gap between management intent and business results is reduced, since there is no handoff between IT and the business; what you see, and what you play with, in the process model is literally what you get.

The real magic comes from using BPM in combination with the *componentized* architecture and a new generation of data modeling and integration tools. Companies now have the ability to access capabilities from their own systems and from their partner firms to create the building blocks of customized business processes that will meet the needs of each customer in each market. A firm can then design and deploy processes that require the involvement of people and systems, within and across a business's boundaries. Collaboration on an intra- and especially interenterprise basis is greatly facilitated and flexibility is hugely enhanced. Networks can be formed for a single customer, and a firm can easily manage many networks at a time.

BPM technology allows designers to make use of software as "components" instead of stovepipe applications and to draw applications together to achieve new processes. A firm can tailor its SRM, CRM, CPFR, e-business, and other systems to match the needs of the most demanding customers. When special requirements are identified, these building blocks can be reorganized into any number of patterns to present a customized solution, without having to start from scratch each time. Large, or branded, nucleus firms can use these technologies to move a supply chain network toward the desired level of connectivity, but smaller players can afford to participate in several networks simultaneously and participate as active and valuable contributors to network performance.

With the technical integration issues all but solved, attention is shifting to the problem of meaning, of making sure that everyone — especially those who come from different industries — understands each message and each activity in the same way. BPM advocates, mostly people who came out of this previous environment and who bear the scars of dealing with all of the complications of systems integration, have found the way to hook together back-end systems with market conditions and the everyday work of administering business contracts. The key ingredient is a standard language for expressing business processes, such as the Business Process Modeling Language (BPML). A new generation of BPM tools is emerging to drive this next stage in the supply chain evolution, and a few path-finding companies are hard at work taking advantage of the breakthrough in a variety of industries.

The business impact is obvious. The IT people see shorter project times and better, faster return on investment, while the important business results move in positive directions. Value to the customer is increased in the form of speed to market with new and innovative products, higher quality, better service, and lower total cost of ownership, while a firm and its network allies build new revenues together. Deployment is so quick and so cheap that payback is often achieved before the project could even have been completed with older technology. More importantly, the linked businesses maintain visibility and control at all times so that customers never get lost in the void. A new bell curve is appearing, one in which the center is skewed to the positive side because more businesses can gain real benefits from their efforts. Those making progress will find anywhere from five to eight points of new profit, but those remaining near the negative end of the longer tail will have trouble sustaining their competitiveness.

This Book Will Serve as a Primer and a Guide to BPM Technology

This book brings together supply chain expertise, practical experience, and firsthand knowledge to explain the deployment of BPM technologies and how to enhance networking efforts across a wide range of industries. It provides a framework, verified by case studies of early adopters, for determining how BPM can become an enabler for advancing into a network enterprise and developing a business case for the required supply chain effort. The book is focused on the business benefits that can be achieved through BPM, but it also introduces sufficient technical detail to plan and execute real, advanced supply chain initiatives.

The chapters will guide any firm, of any size and in any industry, through the supply chain evolution, through the areas that typically stall the effort, and beyond — into a networked enterprise environment and the substantially enhanced results that follow. BPM is not portrayed as a silver bullet. Many businesses have tried similar technologies, often with support from the same systems integrators, and there is no guarantee of success. The same conditions will apply to BPM projects. It is important, therefore, to learn from early, successful implementations, which will be presented in detail. Because it is also crucial to avoid the pitfalls that have stalled others, those issues will be analyzed in some depth.

This book is for anyone who wishes to explore this brave new business world with the help of experienced guides and counselors, to discover what works and what doesn't, and to apply the lessons to their own business network.

ACKNOWLEDGMENTS

The authors would like to thank the many sponsors that helped us drive the research forward by participating in meetings, audio conferences, video conferences, and the Third Wednesday Club. In addition, we would like to recognize:

Bruce Ambler, formerly Senior Manager, IT Software Architecture Strategy, Lucent Technologies, for understanding that unless we extract business process from applications, we will never be able to change as fast as the business wants to change.

Dr. Andreas Baumann, CEO, Webware Experts, for sharing his insights as to how and why it was much easier to develop a pilot using leading-edge, standards-based BPM technology than earlier technologies.

Ron Brown, Consulting and Systems Integration Technical Director, UK Division, CSC, for acting on the possibilities of BPM and BPML, by deploying his e4 architecture to support real systems for real clients.

David Butler, CSC's Research Services, for realizing early that once the ideas of an executable business model developed, the demand for what it promised made it inevitable.

Mark Evans, CIO, Tesoro Petroleum, for seeing how to build on the lessons learned from his first BPM project to turn a point solution into a program of change for the whole organization and for having a clear vision of how IT will deliver value in the future.

Frank Gahse, Senior Product Manager ARIS PPM, IDS Scheer AG, for his insight into the importance of process performance management. He provided us with insight into how businesses can quickly and cost-effectively develop baseline process measurements even when the "as is" process must be reverse engineered out of existing systems. He also demonstrated that real-time performance management can be done with today's technology.

Nigel Green, Head of Service Development EMEA, LINE (UK) Ltd., for his insight into the difference that BPM will make in how companies are run, especially those with global reach.

Jan Gugliotti, Partner, CSC Global Healthcare Solutions, for her insight into how BPM will provide new opportunities and challenges for pharmaceutical companies, as complying with regulation becomes easier and more public.

Rosemary Hartman, Director, Financial Services, CSC Consulting, for her insight into how financial services companies can use BPM and process thinking to transform electronic networks into value networks. Her work provides the basis for many of the ideas presented in the chapter on applying BPM to financial services.

Geoff Hook, BPM Solutions Director, LannerBPM, a division of the Lanner Group, for sharing his experience in using simulation to test business process and supply chain designs and investigate trade-offs in terms of operating rules and resource levels through a "virtual pilot" before implementation in manufacturing and service businesses.

Kris E. Maenhout, Global Solutions Manager, GIS; **Christopher L. Sycalik**, Senior Computer Scientist, GIS; **Gary M. Schall**, Senior Computer Scientist, GIS; and **William J. Tayoun**, Senior Computer Scientist, GIS. This team designed and implemented the BPM solutions for MetaBank that became the intelligent Business Process Manager (iBPM) solution that won the CSC Award for Technical Excellence in 2002. The iBPM solution facilitates the proactive response to business disruption or change through the linkage of a business process to its underlying application and infrastructure components. Through advanced visualization, monitoring, and workflow targeted at the business process, iBPM enables operational excellence by providing the business process owners with a dashboard that allows them to understand how their business is affected by IT failures.

Brian Naaden, CIO of Iowa Telecom, for pointing out how budget pressure can be a helpful driver of innovation and for identifying a way that BPM could deliver project payback in less time than it would have taken to complete the same project in the previous generation of technology.

Piet Opperman, CSC's Research Services, for his diligent review of our draft material and his thoughtful suggestions as to how to improve it.

Joe Pliss, Consulting Software Engineer, LexisNexis, and **Judi Schulz**, LexisNexis, for pointing out that BPM requires a conceptual leap in order to make effective use of the new technologies.

Ian Ramsay, VP of Strategy, Clear Technology, for showing how BPM can liberate staff, especially in paper-intensive industries.

Tom Saxe, VP of Engineering for Systems Architecture and Program Management, Otis Elevator, for helping us to understand how to capture process details in a way that leverages what senior managers know instead of frustrating them.

Steve Scott-Douglas, Director of Solutions, Norwich Union, for showing us how all companies, including financial services firms, are starting to take on many of the supply chain characteristics of manufacturing firms and how BPM tools can help get rid of drudge work and free up staff to spend more time on problem solving.

Dr. George Simpson, Principal Consultant, CSC United Kingdom, for contributing insight into his work on simulation of supply chain processes. He alerted us to the difference between simulating supply chain performance and simulation of the impact of alternative supply chain configurations on market and customers. More importantly, he showed us how to simulate both and to use the results with a BPM solution.

Howard Smith, CTO, CSC Europe, who is a co-founder and co-chair of the Business Process Management Initiative and has developed and deployed BPML, which is a powerful new standard for the expression of complex business processes. He was aware of and involved in this effort way before the rest of us had any idea of what it was or could become. We are grateful to him for his guidance in this and previous Research Services' reports. Together with author Peter Fingar and Ismael Ghalimi, CEO of Intalio, Howard is publishing a book entitled *Business Process Management — The Third Wave* (see www.mkpress.com for details).

Vernon Stinebaker, VP of China Technology and Operations at iUniverse, for the clarity of his search process in looking for BPM technology and his vision of what could be done and relentlessly pursuing it.

John H. Taylor, DuPont Fellow — Information Technology, DuPont, for his assistance in defining the pressure on both IT and the business and for sharing his view of how DuPont's business model and IT strategy have changed to reflect the need for speed and agility.

Ian Walker, Head of CSC's Digital Supply Chain Practice in the United Kingdom, for sharing his work on applying BPM technology to supply chain issues and providing his insight and examples from his work in supply chain strategy across a wide range of supply chains from retaining to process industries.

Terry Williams, Senior Product Manager, LexisNexis, for both being able to see the problem and understanding how BPM could address it.

Linda Wooldridge, CSC's Research Services, for her help in exploring different ways of presenting the ideas of BPM.

THE AUTHORS

Charles Poirier is a partner in the Supply Chain Solutions practice of Computer Sciences Corporation. He is a business veteran with over 40 years of experience helping companies find improvements across their business processing. He is a regular contributor to domestic and international conferences and seminars on subjects ranging from supply chain optimization and electronic commerce to finding hidden values throughout business enterprises and associated partnering opportunities.

His background includes direct management experience in productivity, quality, cost containment, business strategy, mergers and acquisitions, training, sales and marketing, and information technology. His previous publications include *Business Partnering for Continuous Improvement, Supply Chain Optimization, Advanced Supply Chain Management, e-Supply Chain,* and *The Supply Chain Manager's Problem Solver.*

Lynette Ferrara is a leader in CSC's Research and Advisory Services that provides senior business and IT leaders in Fortune 500 businesses with frameworks, tools, and advice on management technology. In her three years at Research Services she has focused on the development and delivery of ideas for transforming a business by effective use of IT. Her advisory work has centered on IT strategy, strategy for mobile and collaborative work, and the application of innovative technologies such as business process management and service-based architecture to issues such as supply chain management. Ms. Ferrara travels the globe speaking to executive audiences and working with clients. She has been interviewed and quoted by the business and IT press in the markets she serves.

Ms. Ferrara develops innovative IT strategies and architectures to improve corporate performance in industry and government. She has served as an IT strategy consultant at CSC Consulting, AT Kearny, and EDS Management Consulting. In all three organizations she had practical leadership and sales responsibilities. For 11 years she served as president of a 70-person firm recognized as a leading provider of executive information systems.

 **Francis Hayden** is based in the London office of CSC's Research Services. He is co-author with Lynette Ferrara and Doug Neal of two reports on business process management and is currently leading research into the future of outsourcing.

His main research interest is in the area of collaboration between business units, businesses, and especially IT and the rest of the business. His three-dimensional Collaboration Framework is now the basis for his consulting and advisory work in outsourcing relationships. Prior to his current work, he researched the way in which the value of IT is assessed and perceived, the way IT vendors are managed, and the relationship between the CIO and CEO.

Prior to joining CSC Research Services, Francis worked as Object Architect for Airbus in the U.K., where he championed the CORBA-based component strategy adopted by the business. As an engineer in the aerodynamics division, he was involved in many different aspects of reengineering with BAe's French, German, and Spanish partners, including work on product data modeling and configuration management. He also represented CSC in the AIT Advanced Configuration Management project.

Francis studied physics at Bristol University, has a postgraduate qualification in theology, and is a qualified teacher with many years of experience.

 **Douglas Neal** is a Research Fellow at CSC's Research Services and is responsible for research into innovation through technology. His interest is in the intersection of strategy, business operations, and technology. Since 2000 he has been researching the emergence of business process management technologies and their impact on business processes.

Other research projects he has undertaken include Deploying Systems at the Customer Interface, Rethinking the Desktop, The Use and Mis-Use of Collaborative Technologies, and Getting Value from Mobile Technologies. Doug's research has included issues of privacy, both the consumers and business to business. His point of view on consumer privacy was published in the October 2000 issue of the *Wilson Quarterly*, the journal of the Woodrow Wilson International Center for Scholars.

Doug is a frequent speaker at executive events around the world. His pioneering work on BPM has made him one of the most knowledgeable speakers in this area, in particular addressing the issue from a business perspective.

Prior to joining CSC Research Services, Doug worked at two international management consulting firms and founded an organization specializing in systems for executive management. He received a B.A. from Haverford College, has conducted special studies at the Ruhr University, and has an A.B.D. from the University of Michigan.

ABOUT APICS

APICS — The Educational Society for Resource Management is a not-for-profit international educational organization recognized as the global leader and premier provider of resource management education and information. APICS is respected throughout the world for its education and professional certification programs. With more than 60,000 individual and corporate members in 20,000 companies worldwide, APICS is dedicated to providing education to improve an organization's bottom line. No matter what your title or need, by tapping into the APICS community you will find the education necessary for success.

APICS is recognized globally as:

- The source of knowledge and expertise for manufacturing and service industries across the entire supply chain
- The leading provider of high-quality, cutting-edge educational programs that advance organizational success in a changing, competitive marketplace
- A successful developer of two internationally recognized certification programs, Certified in Production and Inventory Management (CPIM) and Certified in Integrated Resource Management (CIRM)
- A source of solutions, support, and networking for manufacturing and service professionals

For more information about APICS programs, services, or membership, visit www.apics.org or contact APICS Customer Support at (800) 444-2742 or (703) 354-8851.

*Free value-added materials available from
the Download Resource Center at www.jrosspub.com*

At J. Ross Publishing we are committed to providing today's professional with practical, hands-on tools that enhance the learning experience and give readers an opportunity to apply what they have learned. That is why we offer free ancillary materials available for download on this book and all participating Web Added Value™ publications. These online resources may include interactive versions of material that appears in the book or supplemental templates, worksheets, models, plans, case studies, proposals, spreadsheets and assessment tools, among other things. Whenever you see the WAV™ symbol in any of our publications, it means bonus materials accompany the book and are available from the Web Added Value Download Resource Center at www.jrosspub.com.

Downloads available for *The Networked Supply Chain: Applying Breakthrough BPM Technology to Meet Relentless Customer Demands* consist of networked supply chain and BPM technology examples, assessment tools, illustrations, and enabling models.

GO BEYOND SUPPLY CHAIN BY CREATING A NETWORKED ENTERPRISE

The Networked Enterprise Has Become the Goal

Over the past ten years, many businesses have realized that they need to belong to a successful networked enterprise — even though very few of them have achieved their ambition. The vision is that enterprises would link together and collaborate to ensure that real customer needs and actual business requirements would drive them all toward optimized operating conditions. By integrating their efforts to focus on customer or consumer satisfaction, the linked firms would have the right products available at the point of need, eliminate goods and services that do not sell, reduce inventory, force out extraneous operating costs, optimize the use of joint assets, and build new revenues together. Business partners would come together, share important information, analyze their business/value propositions, and better understand their core operating processes. They could then go in search of ways to improve and ultimately transform their linked supply chains in a cooperative manner.

The Plan Was to Evolve from Business Process Improvement Through Supply Chain Optimization to the Networked Enterprise

Virtually every firm of any size was already laboring under some form of process improvement effort during this time frame, so the obvious strategy was to bring together the best ideas and practices from these efforts and merge them under an umbrella initiative, which was usually called the *supply chain*. The early focus was on establishing alliances with important suppliers and customers and then working with those allies to enhance the supply chain process steps. The core ideas of the supply chain, the value chain, or interenterprise cooperation quickly became recognized and accepted as an important business process improvement approach. Entirely new titles, leadership, and staffing structures began to appear, and organizations moved forward to find the expected benefits.

The new cadre of experts began their supply chain optimization work by drawing maps of how the processing was conducted, paying particular attention to the points of handoff, where inefficiencies typically occur. From receiving orders to buying supplies, making products, creating services, and delivering to customers, attention was focused on how to complete that work as effectively and as efficiently as possible. Three flows were described by these process maps: movement of products and services, information, and finances. Most companies that paid serious attention to supply chain processing in this way found early gains and added a few points of profit to their earnings.

Then business partners went in search of higher levels of savings and profits. As they discovered and implemented improvements, they progressed toward advanced supply chain management techniques, which required the use and application of external resources. Cycle times, for example, were approached on a network basis and reduced to industry-best levels so that customer needs could be met much more quickly and cash flows could be dramatically improved for the participants.

Other Industries Are Just Discovering the Need for Supply Chain Excellence

Entire industries, such as healthcare and financial services, which were slow to adopt these ideas because the notion of a "supply chain" is usually associated with manufacturing, are just now discovering the value of supply chain optimization. Insurance companies are stepping up to the challenge of automating claims processing. Industry traders, custodial banks, and financial markets are under pressure from regulators and institutional customers to achieve what is called "straight through processing" between firms when they have not even integrated people and systems within their own four walls. In healthcare, payer/provider organizations are seeking new ways to cut costs while maintaining and improving the quality of care.

In an early step toward improvement in the insurance industry, Lloyd's of London is leading an industry effort to improve the handling of underwriting among the hundreds of brokers who currently employ dozens of couriers, who carry large claims files under their arms and go looking for underwriters who have backed a specific policy or risk. Lloyd's has built on a claims-processing system already in use by a cluster of insurers and linked that system with a new document repository to cut the costs of processing complex industrial claims by half. "The repository not only lets brokers, underwriters, and adjusters digitally access the information they need, it also provides tools such as online chat, instant messaging, and video-over-Internet protocol for real-time collaboration" (Kontzer, 2002, p. 36).

Most Supply Chain Optimization Projects Were Successful in the Early Stages and Then Ground to a Halt

Most business organizations were rewarded in some manner for their early supply chain optimization efforts, and a few, such as Wal-Mart with Procter & Gamble, Sainsbury with Nestlé, and DuPont with Ford, even advanced into a form of advanced supply chain management networked enterprise. But broader analysis of results across industries, markets, and companies shows a distinctly checkered pattern. Pioneers like Wal-Mart, Boeing, Cisco, and Intel have persevered for half a decade or more and secured industry-dominant positions as a result of their efforts while others have become disillusioned and withdrawn from the fray altogether. The gap between the leaders and followers, based on our research of over 300 firms, can now be as much as one to two years in elapsed time or five to eight points in annual profit, and it could spell the difference between long-term success and failure.

The majority of efforts, however, fall somewhere in the middle of this success spectrum, achieving some early success but reaching the point of diminishing returns or stalling for lack of resources or continued support. It was not hard to find the early savings; they came from better purchasing and sourcing, logistics, storage, product delivery, and management of inventory. An early rule of thumb was that for an intense effort of at least three years, three points of new profit could be added to the bottom line. But when firms tried to find more savings by continuing to leverage their buying power and using electronic commerce to reach higher levels of success, most efforts began to deliver fewer returns and many stalled altogether. It became clear to many of these organizations that they had run up against a wall of some kind and that something new would be required for them to climb over it.

As shown in Figure 1.1, supply chain efforts progress through five distinct levels on the way to full network agility. This evolution will be considered in detail in subsequent chapters, but the important point that emerges from our industry samples is that the majority of firms are still working on intraenterprise issues. The reality is that after a decade or more of trying, most firms have become bogged down somewhere between level 2 and 3 of the supply chain evolution. Only the real innovators have poked through or jumped over the wall to start work on the external environment and embark on the road to levels 4 and 5. Our research also shows that even these innovators will typically have only one or two business units that have done so; the business in general is still laboring to get past level 2.

This, by the way, is a model worth imitating. Finishing the work needed in level 2 by getting the internal house in order is extremely important, but a firm is well advised to move at least one business unit further forward, to prove the validity of the concepts and to determine how collaboration and technology can be used with a limited number of business partners to develop new business models and innovative value propositions that can lead to market dominance.

The Leaders Have a Number of Things in Common

The genuine network value chains that have so far been built by the likes of Dell, Cisco, Wal-Mart, and Tesco share a number of features. The first is that they tend to be dominated and driven by one company — what

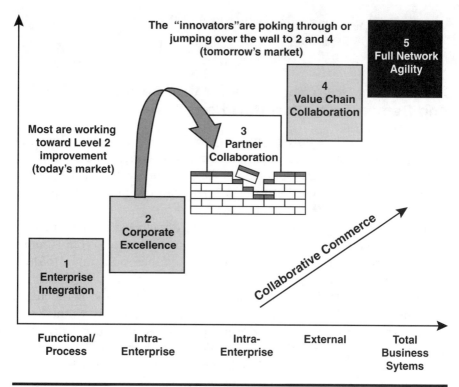

Figure 1.1   The Supply Chain Evolution

we call a *nucleus firm* — which is big enough to impose decisions on the other participants and committed enough to propel the whole network toward success. They tend to have a culture that encourages working with others, and it helps to be a new company with little process or technology baggage to offload.

Among all the other diverse success factors, there is also a common technology ingredient. All of these companies successfully persuaded their trading partners to adopt the same technology and to exchange information using de facto standards based on technologies such as electronic data interchange, RosettaNet, and XML. All the solutions are proprietary at some level, and, most important, they provide a sustainable advantage because they would be extremely expensive and time consuming to copy. Previous generations of e-business technologies, built by plugging together off-the-shelf solutions, tried to reduce the time and cost of constructing networks, but they could not provide the same level of supply chain improvement.

The Leaders Have Shown That It Can Be Done — And Demonstrated Just How Hard It Is

Supply chain work is now fully recognized and accepted as a business process improvement technique, but the gap between leaders and followers is significant. The opportunity for savings is clearly genuine, but the leaders have shown that the real prize can only be claimed under certain very particular circumstances.

Today's customers are relentless. They demand products and services that are better, cheaper, faster, and super-pleasing. What is more, the only reward for meeting their demands is the opportunity to do it again next year. We are caught on a relentless treadmill of business improvement — tempered only by the thought that the competition faces the same challenges. Can it really be true that the only winners will be those that happen to cluster around a successful nucleus firm and those that opt for a winning combination of technologies? We believe companies of any size can work with a nucleus firm or other businesses to create a market differentiation, through the use of emerging technologies which we will consider and discuss in detail.

Enter Business Process Management: The Fast, Affordable Network Solution

This book is about a breakthrough technology — business process management (BPM) — that has changed the competitive business landscape. BPM affords businesses the means to manage processes across systems, people, and organizations, providing visibility and control over each instance of those processes right across the supply chain network. For the first time, all parties will be able to track the real flow of goods, money, and information from end to end of the chain. Customers will be able to inquire about the state of the process, no matter which partners happen to be handling the current tasks at that moment. With previous technologies, this capability was feasible only if companies adopted the same technologies and invested vast sums of money and time in constructing the network relationships. This burden of construction work made such networks enormously rigid. They could be changed, but only with another huge investment of time and money. With BPM, these networks are suddenly much easier to design and deploy, and changes are often just a click of the mouse away.

A BPM system is not an application in the conventional sense. Nor is it just a piece of infrastructural plumbing; it does much more than glue systems together like conventional middleware. It is somewhere in between the two conditions. Like the conductor of an orchestra, it makes no noise itself, but it directs and coordinates the work of the real players. The players in this case are the existing information technology (IT) systems like enterprise resource planning, customer relationship management, and e-procurement applications, or, even better, components carved out of them so that they can play in any way the business requires. A key benefit of BPM technology is that it is no longer necessary to replace your older systems. What we commonly refer to as our "legacy" can be converted into a set of genuine assets, made to do completely new things, and managed at a much finer level of control than previously possible.

A breakthrough capability of a BPM system is that the BPM software engine can directly execute business processes and connect them with existing and future systems. Previously, business process descriptions were just high-level diagrams on the conference room wall or in a thick notebook. Moving from the high-level diagrams to running systems was difficult, time consuming, and sometimes imprecise.

Now business processes can be described in new languages that the BPM engine can read and execute without further translation or development. Examples of these languages are Business Process Modeling Language (BPML), developed by the Business Process Management Initiative (BPMI.org), an international consortium of 160 companies, and Business Process Execution Language (BPEL), initiated by Microsoft, IBM, and BEA and now taken over by a Technical Committee of OASIS (http://www.oasis-open.org/committees/tc_home.php?wg_abbrev= wsbpel).

The critical feature of BPM systems for supply chain initiatives, and the key that will unlock all the programs that are stalled at level 2, is that they are designed to communicate with each other. Two companies only need to install and connect compatible BPM systems and they can instantly share the management of a joint process simply by dropping the same model into both of them. With the advent of BPM technology, the race for the networked enterprise has begun in earnest.

Traditional Nucleus Firms Have Used BPM to Solve Problems That Were Intractable with Older Technology

The big advantage that nucleus firms establish is that they only have to trade with a fixed set of partners, and they can dictate the single technology standard by which they will do so. Even so, many of these firms come across problems that have been too difficult to solve until BPM technology appeared on the scene. Each of the following projects achieved payback before a similar effort using older technology could have even been completed.

- **iUniverse**: This start-up was formed in 2000 with the objective of dramatically reducing the cost and time required to publish an initial run of hard-copy books and to fulfill follow-on orders — even if for only one book — within three to five days. It used the Internet to significantly expand its ability to reach and interact with potential authors, but when it started to do the same thing with printers and catalog companies, it ran into a rat's nest of complexity. Every printer wanted things differently, and every catalog company wanted things its own special way. While it was theoretically possible to write separate Active Server Pages to meet the special requirements, the labor costs were prohibitive, especially in keeping pace with changes. Now, using a BPM system (in this case Intalio's n3), each printer and catalog company is just a specific variant of a more general process, which can be tweaked within the Intalio visual design tool. Changes are made to the process diagrams and no coding is required.

- **Norwich Union**: In a pilot of BPM using Tranzax from Clear Technologies, Norwich Union was able to demonstrate the potential ability to automate many manual tasks in claims processing. As a result, it saw the means to cut the cycle time for claims processing and eliminate errors in calculating payments due to customers and other insurance companies. Just as importantly, it is expected that job satisfaction among claims processors will improve and that staff turnover could be cut. Not only did the new technology show how most of the boring work could be eliminated, it turned the job into something that worked well and made money for the company.

- **LexisNexis:** This legal, news, and business information service sells a vast array of information to the legal, corporate, and government markets in both on-line and hard-copy formats. Historically, this complex service has been sold only to very large organizations. Recently, it has looked to expand sales to medium and smaller organizations. It needed a way to connect and perform error checking on a series of systems that had never been designed to work together. The solution was to use Intalio's n3 BPM system and to make use of the way that n3 carries information about the process along with the process as it executes. This change meant that each system could use the same information instead of having its own source, and the underlying cause of many of the errors was eliminated with a stroke.

Other Smaller Businesses Can Now Join the Party

While benefits from BPM to the nucleus firms make exciting news, the big breakthrough will be for the thousands of nonnucleus firms that have to trade with several major companies. Until now, these firms had to adopt costly technology and customize it for every network they joined. Thanks to BPM, they can now interact as full process partners without investing in unique technology for every network.

This may be the first supply chain book that is not just for and about the supply chain giants. It is for every company looking to move to the next level of business improvement. Some examples follow:

- Tesoro Petroleum used BPM to leverage its investment in SAP, developing a new system to manage the provisioning of ships in less than four months and without customizing the SAP itself. SAP alone had delivered a 65-screen system that required one year of training to use, hardly feasible when the average dockworker stays in the job for less than four months. As a result, ships left the dock before anyone could log their order and generate an invoice. Tesoro used a BPM system from FuegoTech to automate most of the manual screen updates and to provide dockworkers with a simple portal to log orders and to check credit. As a result, it could generate invoices at provisioning time, which took 90 days out of the payment cycle.

- Iowa Telecom used BPM to automate long-distance provisioning, which involved the use of several systems. Using BPM technology from FuegoTech, it was able to automate 80 percent of the manual transactions, and customer requests to change long-distance providers that once took minutes are now completed in seconds. The BPM project cost about one-third as much as more mainstream application integration technology, and the reduced head count paid for the project in eight months — four months before the more conventional approach could have even delivered a solution.

Best Process Management Will Replace Best Practice

Nucleus firms are very keen on the notion of "best practice," as if there were one way of doing things that fit every situation. Smaller players already know that there is no such thing; they just have to operate the way their bigger suppliers and customers demand — and if that means doing it five different ways, then so be it. BPM technology will improve their lives by making it easy to introduce and to manage process variants, and in the end even the big players will realize that if they can give customers what they really want, everyone involved will gain a competitive advantage. With BPM, your firm can now meet the most demanding customer requirements; the secret is to master the technologies and management techniques before your competitors do.

BPM systems allow any firm, regardless of size or complexity, to construct or participate in a supply chain network similar to those used by such leaders as Adaptec, Boeing, Cisco, Colgate-Palmolive, Dell, Hewlett-Packard, Intel, Procter & Gamble, Solectron, Toyota, and Wal-Mart. A firm can now tailor its supplier relationship management, customer relationship management, collaborative planning, forecasting, and replenishment, and other improvement efforts to match the needs of the most demanding customers. A typical example illustrates the potential improvement.

At a large high-tech manufacturing company, sourcing and fulfillment have been difficult because its enterprise resource planning (ERP) system provides only standard processes for interacting with its partners, regardless of their different characteristics or the different kinds of product that they produce. Introducing variants would require the ERP vendor to customize its package and to maintain the variations in each new release. Even then, the processes would still be embedded deep within the application with little or no room for change.

The standard process was not perfect in any case. For example, when an order came in, it would be validated in a strict sequence. If there was an error in the part code, it was immediately sent back to the originator for correction without looking ahead to see if there might also be a problem with the address or the billing number. This could result in a large number of iterations before an order could finally be placed.

A decision was taken to move the definition of the order process outside the ERP system into an environment that was designed to handle the complexity of separate processes for each customer. The order management capabilities of the ERP system are now invoked from a BPM system (from Intalio), under the control of a process that was designed by the business staff responsible for that area.

This shift in responsibility, to the people who knew the business, was a strong attraction. Previously, important details of exactly how an order should work for a specific company and product would get lost in compiling the general business requirements, and business users were continually frustrated by the fact that the system would not do what they really needed.

Sourcing from Catalogs Will Demonstrate the Impact of BPM on the Supply Chain

In a specific area of potential improvement, BPM will enhance sourcing benefits without requiring the tightly coupled systems integration that is difficult to achieve and often harder to maintain. By reducing the time needed to build and maintain catalogs, while integrating with existing systems, BPM eliminates the barriers to implementing e-procurement for both buyer and seller. Suppliers can use their existing IT systems to provide real-time links to their multiple vendors or allow their authorized employees to search the Web and choose the best vendor based on prices for the day or transaction. They can establish their own rules for suggesting vendors and logistics providers, while creating a data flow back to their internal billing systems. Most importantly, they can integrate the full power of supplier systems, such as those provided by Staples, Home Depot, and W. W. Grainger, into their applications. Their customers get up-to-the-minute availability information and can locate hard-to-find goods via the Internet. The business can then integrate its back office systems to harvest the transaction cost savings. It becomes a typical win–win BPM situation, with the supply chain becoming a thread of interactions, which can be viewed and managed in real time by anyone with the appropriate authority.

BPM Is Prescribed for Internal Use in the First Instance

BPM is invariably applied on an internal basis first, to solve a problem that was insoluble with other technologies. Capability can then be offered to external supply chain partners to coordinate with their systems. A firm that has successfully used BPM can provide it to selected business allies that have less demand for it internally but need to be integrated into the overall processing. The benefits will enhance any improvement effort, regardless of the firm, its scale, or industry practices, and lead to a networked position of dominance for the allied constituents.

This Book Is for You, the Manager

As a final reminder, we expect IT people to find this book helpful, but it is really aimed at business managers. Previous technologies have claimed to be user friendly, but reality has shown that most applications that address serious business problems require the skills and experience of IT people to do anything with them. Your IT staff will be needed to link your business models to your processing and underlying systems, but with BPM you will participate in the development of the process model, which in the end is what manages the whole process and all the systems that support it. Forget the gap between intent and execution; what you see will be what you get. BPM systems even provide tools for simulating a process before you deploy it.

This book is your road map to what is possible and what is not. It provides case studies of companies that have already successfully used BPM in industries as diverse as heavy manufacturing, consumer products, and financial services. It is designed to provide you with the insight to select your first project, to manage it to success, and to get started on your way to productive participation in the networked enterprise of your choice.

2

BPM OPENS THE DOOR TO NETWORKED ENTERPRISES

Business process management (BPM) is a "disruptive technology" — a technology that will profoundly transform markets and alter long-term customer relationships by changing what is possible and affordable in everyday business relationships. Those who adopt the technology will discover that once-elusive supply chain networks can now be built more easily and cheaply than ever before. Even small businesses can participate in multiple network enterprises and can find ways to build networks that meet the needs of the most demanding customers at ever lower price points. The requirement is for your business to quickly master this new technology. To help in that endeavor, this chapter provides an overview of how BPM works.

BPM Links Businesses Together

As companies of all sizes, in virtually every industry, have sought the means to bring higher levels of success to their governing metrics, most discovered they needed to link up with at least a few important external companies (on the upstream and downstream sides), in some form of network arrangement, to gain access to information that was critical to their operations. Automobile makers, for example, found that it was impossible to offer short-term cycles of delivery for new vehicles without the cooperation of tier 1 and tier 2 suppliers in providing nonconstrained flows of materials and subassemblies to their factories. It became a sort of business jigsaw puzzle, in which progress was made but no one firm had all of the crucial pieces of data to complete the picture of optimized conditions.

Virtual communication loomed as the Achilles' heel of a firm's desire to attain a viable position within many networked enterprises. Supply chain efforts around the world were particularly perplexed by how to overcome this central issue, as the constituents continued to find savings but became stymied by how to work together in a manner that would lead to superior performance while gaining a distinctive differentiation in the eyes of the desired customers or consumers.

BPM has emerged as the missing piece to this business puzzle, especially for those firms seeking further advancement with their supply chains. BPM became the breakthrough in the ability to manage the work of people, systems, and organizations in a collaborative manner. It became the technical means that made use of software accessibility as a component of software functions, instead of having to cope with gaining access to stovepipe applications. BPM greatly facilitates interenterprise communication and further process improvement. As shown in Figure 2.1, it becomes the thread of interaction. Users have discovered that the tool, moreover, makes getting the internal house in order (level 2) much more feasible before a firm seeks partnerships with other, and often much larger, external business partners (level 3 and beyond).

BPM is a set of technologies that provides business with the means to manage processes across the supply chain network. Central to its enhancing ability, BPM will:

- Provide visibility and control as it tracks every process thread, doing so by orchestrating the activities of people, systems, and participation with other companies
- Reduce the gap between management intent and process execution, since the process model generates the executable code that manages the activities of participants

With BPM, all parties in a supply chain network can track the real-time flow of goods, money, and information across the network. They can also answer customer questions on the state of the process, no matter who is handling the process at a given point in time. This capability was

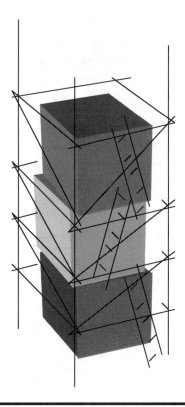

Figure 2.1   Supply Chain Becomes a Thread of Interactions

previously only possible if companies adopted the same technologies and invested lots of money and time in building the network connectivity. These networks could be changed, but at a time and cost similar to what were required for the initial project. With BPM, these networks are suddenly much easier and cheaper to design, deploy, and change.

BPM culminates in the designing of systems to integrate business processing across people in their own domain, by connecting them with each other so process components can be integrated to create manageable distributed processing. It extends externally with the cooperation of supply chain partners agreeing to collaborate through an accepted language and conducting business in an integrated manner.

As one considers the role of BPM, it is first and foremost a business issue. After an extended period of business expansion, most companies are under severe pressure to meet their financial objectives. Many of these firms are seeking short-term as well as long-term improvement to operational and economic performance, with most of the pressure being applied to the former area. BPM assists in the response to this pressure from customer and competitors, and the need for dramatic organizational change, by creating the kind of easier connectivity that supply chain partners have been seeking.

BPM must be viewed as a powerful enabler of process improvement during these times, starting at the beginning of the supply chain and proceeding to a logical conclusion of the processing with customer satisfaction. BPM is then used to manage the end-to-end process, which crosses internal and external company boundaries, ending with the end consumer. Transition to this brave new world requires a new technology that integrates crucial data between different business partners and different technologies. When applied, the features of BPM include:

- Elimination of unnecessary work
- Automation of routine work
- Empowerment of the right people, so they can focus on problem solving, innovation, making sense of the vast amount of information now available to them, or listening to customers
- Deployment of customized processes in response to customer demands
- Support of process collaboration across business boundaries

Technology Becomes the Business Enabler

With an understanding that BPM is essentially a business-enhancing tool, attention should turn next to understanding the key linkage between BPM and information technology (IT). As can be seen in Figure 2.2, it was originally presumed that the IT evolution across the supply chain progression would move logically from providing point solutions,

	Levels 1 & 2	Level 3	Level 4	Level 5
Information Technology	Point Solutions Internal Stovepipe Conditions	Linked Intranets Corp. Strategy/ Architecture	Internet-Based Extranet Shared Capabilities	Full Network Communication System Shared Architecture Planning

Figure 2.2   The Flow of Technology Improvement Across the Supply Chain Evolution

pursued under internal stovepipe conditions, to creating more beneficial results. It was supposed to move to linked intranet actions, which combined corporate strategy with the architectures being applied. Next, the firms would progress, with the help of external partners, to build an extranet, using the Internet as the heart of this construction, and shared capabilities would lead to a superior value chain. Finally, the level of full network connectivity would be achieved through system shared architecture planning.

The conventional wisdom was that it was about putting the right applications and infrastructure in place to support improved business techniques — supplier relationship management, sales and operations planning, advanced planning and scheduling, enterprise resource planning (ERP), customer relationship management, enterprise application integration, advanced supply chain management, and so forth. It was also to be about sharing data standards and moving logically by requiring external partners to accept the direction of the more powerful channel master or nucleus firm. Early in the game, the thinking was that difficulties stemmed from softer issues, grounded in culture, management style, or lack of leadership. These factors are important, but the larger issue is how to follow the threads of communication across the linked partners. That requires an enabling technology and learning how to collaborate with willing and trusted supply chain partners. It also requires a guiding mission or purpose to overcome the natural inhibitions and to build a strong business model, which is compelling in the eyes of the customer and can lead to optimized conditions. That vision must come through an internal collaboration between those responsible for IT and those responsible for business management.

Another realization is that it was not just a case of putting the right applications in place. As can be seen in Figure 2.3, that was done, and the result was a littering of the supply chain landscape with a plethora of applications and no holistic solutions.

The complication is that collaboration between companies typically requires some form of integrating model. Because of the typical political problem associated with firms not wanting to take direction from external sources, some sort of federated model became necessary. Even a simple order fulfillment process can require the integration of five different systems applications, as illustrated in Figure 2.4 for purchase order processing. With so many systems at work, a federated model is required to integrate across the various systems from, say, a major chemical company and tier 1 or tier 2 suppliers to an automotive original

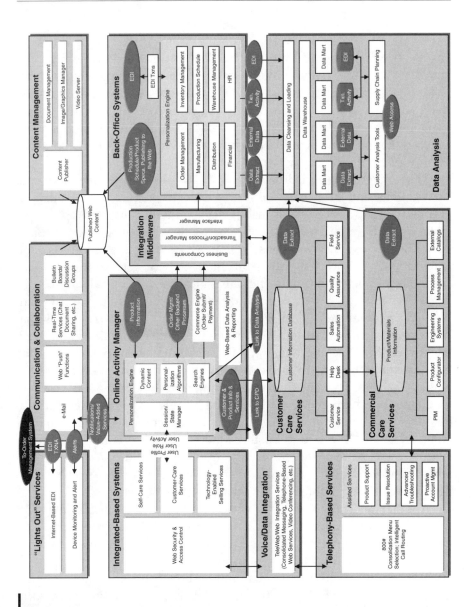

Figure 2.3 Multiple Applications Do Not Provide Holistic Solutions (Source: CSC's Research Services)

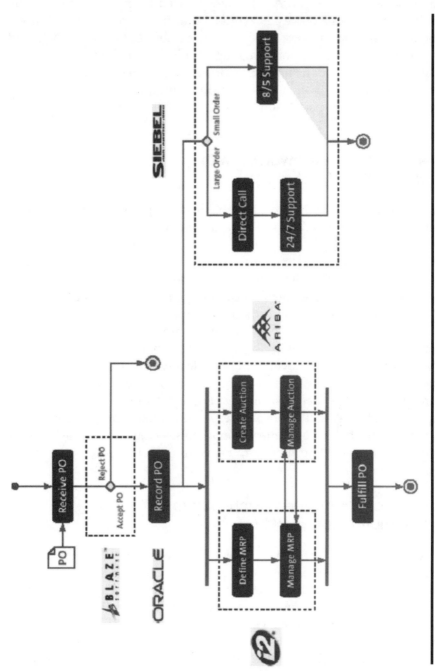

Figure 2.4   Software Involved in Purchase Order Processing (Source: Intalio, Inc.)

equipment manufacturer. A rich, standardized language that could describe the business processes would be a crucial advantage. Process languages such as Business Process Management Language (BPML) and Business Process Execution Language (BPEL) have emerged with the mathematics that can facilitate this processing and enable the necessary information exchange. In a large-scale interenterprise network, the players can function as peers, eliminating the political considerations.

Central Ideas Are Involved with BPM and Supply Chain

At the core of the ability to move beyond supply chain by creating a networked enterprise are some basic fundamentals. First, successful execution will be directed by means of a mutually agreed upon, sensible strategy and differentiating process model, not by agreeing to share software application. The objective is to reduce the lag between management's strategic intentions and implementation and deployment of business processing. With the cooperation of business unit leaders and the IT staff, BPM then becomes the technique to manage the necessary work in an effective manner, for the benefit of all supply chain constituents. BPM, moreover, will provide a way to integrate the linked business process steps to respond more quickly and accurately to company and customer needs, while leveraging existing IT infrastructures, especially ERP, to make concrete responses better than any competing network. The challenge for most firms is to select an area of the business and build a compelling model, to prove the validity of the concepts.

Service or Component Architecture Is the Foundation of BPM

As mentioned, BPM provides sophisticated tools to reconfigure and redeploy your existing IT systems to meet the ever-changing demands of your customers. But BPM would not be quite as easy to implement without another important technology breakthrough: the move to service or componentized architectures, supported by nearly all the major enterprise software vendors such as IBM, SAP, JD Edwards, Oracle, Microsoft, and Siebel. What this means is that the major software suppliers are providing greater access to their software at the component level.

Figure 2.5 Software and System Components (Source: CSC's Research Services)

Firms such as SAP and Siebel once fiercely protected the internals of their software. They are now opening their software so that customers can swiftly integrate it with other applications to support an end-to-end process.

Newer architectures, Web services, and Internet-based applications then provide explicit standards for developing plug-and-play components, as illustrated in Figure 2.5, using such standards as Web Services Description Language (WSDL), simple object application protocol (SOAP), and universal description, discovery, and integration (UDDI). Today, there are a number of proven methods to create *components* within your older legacy systems, like Java connectivity and existing middleware, and then to interact with your channel partners.

The question becomes how you manage these components to produce a reliable business process. The answer is that BPM technologies can be used to make the pieces work together. BPM can be used to find the real chunks of necessary data from the system, whereas the legacy systems preclude making the data available for user needs. BPM arrives as a technical breakthrough in this environment. It makes visibility and control possible, where they were not feasible before, and it can be used to manage the components — a key to making changes quickly. Since the components can be accessed across cyberspace, this capability is extended across people, systems, and organizations, closing the gap between management intent and execution by means of directly executable business process models. All of this is accomplished, as illustrated in Figure 2.6, while leveraging your existing IT infrastructure.

At this point, we should pause and consider the capabilities afforded

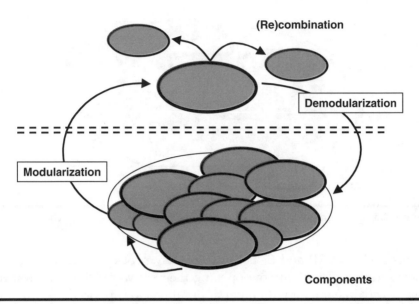

Figure 2.6 Software and System Components with BPM (Source: CSC's Research Services)

by BPM. First, the application of BPM allows a firm to keep track of the important process threads in the end-to-end supply chain. With its use, you do not need to force-feed multiple organizations one set of applications that must be kept in sync . The use of BPML, to be discussed below, allows a firm to support multiple variations of a process.

The advantages come from the ability to use BPM to manage components of each firm's IT assets, which is the key to making necessary changes rapidly. Existing IT assets are accessed through a wide range of connection technologies and then managed by BPM to support the precise processes needed for each customer. BPM facilitates process management across many supply chain network constituents, enabling reengineering and redesign and bringing returns in less time than trying to implement with older technologies.

A Process Language for Defining the Business Components

There is one necessary ingredient in this new world of connectivity: the enabling communication language. Most of today's BPM technologies

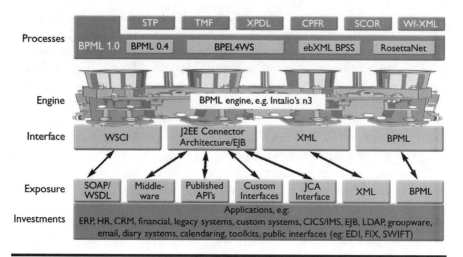

Figure 2.7 The Role of BPML in Creating Business Connectivity (Source: Intalio, Inc. and CSC's Research Services)

use a mixture of proprietary and standards-based technologies, while businesses are forced to adopt a common BPM system if they want to share the management of a joint process. In the brave new future, any BPM system will be able to collaborate with any other using a standard process description language. While the final standard has not yet emerged, the two leading formats, BPML and BPEL, share a common core based on mathematics and computer science.

BPML was developed by the Business Process Management Initiative (BPMI.org), a 160-company international consortium. Essentially, BPML is a language for computer systems rather than people. Process designers tend to work with graphical representations, whereas business managers think in terms of metrics and process outcomes. Different disciplines will interact with BPM systems using tool sets that "speak their language" and in terms that are relevant to their industry. Indeed, BPML implementations will bring process management to existing and future investments. As shown in Figure 2.7, BPML supports a wide variety of evolving standards. IBM has announced BPEL, which is a subset of BPML, developed in conjunction with Oracle, BEA, and Microsoft. In April 2003, an OASIS Technical Committee was formed to guide development of BPEL.

Shared process initiatives, including straight through processing (STP) and collaborative planning, forecasting, and replenishment (CPFR), can move through processing enabled by BPML, including that which uses program languages such as WSFL, Microsoft's XLANG, and RosettaNet. The BPM engine orchestrates the use of multiple Web services by providing the connections to other technology standards, such as single components like Web Services Choreography Interface (WSCI) and services like SOAP and WSDL. BPML subsumes all other languages, and options then appear, to exchange processing data, or drop down to interface with other constituents and decide how to connect the things you want into your business process systems. This move leads to data integration and many collaborative possibilities. Importantly, you will know in the processing what you can send and get back and how multiple Web services will react and work together.

To support the definition and execution of any business process, BPML must be semantically rich enough to represent material flows, information flows, and business commitments. It must be able to support the different process paradigms in common use across different industries and unify the various distributed computing models that underpin existing and emerging middleware. It should represent combinations of business-to-business collaboration and enterprise application integration. It must also consolidate workflow processing with automated procedures, while allowing the integration of hosted applications, such as Web services.

In addition to accomplishing these advantages, BPML is designed to:

- Expose existing back-end systems and software application logic as business processes
- Allow a process engine to integrate with existing messaging and transaction middleware and database management systems
- Support the interchange of processes off-line (packaged processes) as well as on-line (peer to peer)
- Enable processes to react to events and adapt to changing business requirements in real time
- Simplify the management of interactions between processes running on disparate systems and across different business domains
- Enable the rapid development and deployment of new processes, by combining existing process components into new value-added processes
- Enable IT to combine best-of-breed solutions, such as visual process modeling tools, process engines, process management systems, and process analysis tools

BPML becomes the meta-language that offers a generic execution model for business processes which can be translated into more concrete and specific languages that apply to vertical domains within an industry. Examples of industry process templates, expected to be expressed in BPML and adapted by end users for strategic advantage, include:

- Retail: CPFR
- Securities trading: Financial Products Markup Language (FpML)
- Finance: Complying with the T=1 Securities and Exchange Commission regulations and straight through processing
- Telecommunications: Service provisioning and management (the TeleManagement Forum)
- Manufacturing: Managing product life cycles (Standard for the Exchange of Product Model Data [STEP])
- High technology: Reducing inventory levels (RosettaNet, Supply Chain Operations Reference [SCOR] model)
- Insurance: Supporting Health Insurance Portability Act regulation (Global Insurance Standards [ACORD])

In essence, BPM systems will become process nodes, connecting businesses together in the design and execution of their processing. Specific industries will form subnetworks with specialized kinds of collaboration, but ultimately everyone will be connected. And the beauty will be that it will not cost a king's ransom to establish or participate.

And what can businesses expect in the way of results? BPM eliminates the need to depend on monolithic, stovepipe technology applications, reducing the lag between management intent and execution, by means of a directly executable business model. It does so while leveraging the firm's existing IT infrastructure, especially ERP, and making the results more concrete and responsive. As a concluding thought, it also becomes a business imperative on the way to optimized conditions, and if your firm does not do it, a competing firm can be expected to step in and take your place. The chart displayed in Figure 2.7 is not about technology. It is about making better business decisions.

Conclusions

There are a few business requirements if a firm wants to take advantage of the breakthrough offered by BPM as it moves beyond supply chain and into network participation. A firm needs to rethink its management and technology strategies. It needs to reorchestrate its work with supply chain partners, agreeing to collaboratively apply BPM as the enabling engine in the linked processing. The network then becomes the concept that drives advanced supply chain efforts, and total optimization across the end-to-end linkage becomes a feasible objective.

The features of this emerging BPM enabled network will be such that firms do not have to adopt the same or shared applications or infrastructure. Rather, they can all agree on BPM as the enabler. The supply chain partners can then communicate using multiple standards, but one standard will be better for all participants. With BPM, any business can become a Cisco or Intel. The actual benefits of collaborative process management in the supply chain domain are still being proven, but preliminary studies and the work done by some of the leading firms in the retail and high-technology areas suggest that the benefits could be as significant as those achieved to reach level 3 or 4. This implies that another 15 to 20 percent of profit could be added.

BPM offers a solution that operates at the business level, integrates supply chain analytics and process performance metrics, and allows a consolidated analysis and subsequent management of value, up and down the supply chain. In the process, it becomes the key tool to integrate what were once several independent procedures — value analysis, process analysis, quality management, and costing — into one analysis. That is the essence of BPM enhancement.

3

SUPPLY CHAIN WORK IS PART OF A LONG HISTORY OF BUSINESS IMPROVEMENT

Supply chain work is the latest step in a sequence of highly visible improvement efforts. First in line was total quality management, in which Edwards Deming, Joe Juran, Phil Crosby, Armand Feigenbaum, and others showed how an emphasis on quality could lead to dramatically better performance, lower overall costs, and happier customers. Next came business process reengineering, where Michael Hammer and James Champy pointed out how nonvalue-adding steps could be eliminated from processes and solutions could be delivered more quickly and with fewer personnel. Continuous process improvement emerged from those efforts and was followed by an emphasis on end-to-end processing that became defined as supply chain management.

Pictures like Figure 3.1, based on Michael Porter's value chain model, were often used to describe the linear processing that was said to take place across such a supply chain, starting with supplies and moving on through manufacture to a business customer. Firms sought the means to drive out costs by challenging the methods and procedures in each link.

The purpose was to find all the hidden value that had eluded companies during their previous excursions into quality, reengineering, and pro-

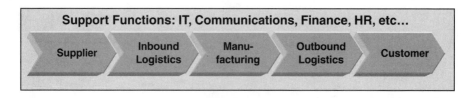

Figure 3.1 The Traditional View of Supply Chain

cess improvement. Beginning internally, teams were dispatched to find ways of breaking down the typical barriers to internal cooperation and to promote the sharing of information and best practices. With some gains in the bag, firms then turned their attention to the external environment and began collaborating with a few supply chain allies and trusted business partners to find even more value. The picture of the supply chain was typically expanded at the downstream end, as in Figure 3.2, to include a distribution center, a retail store, and end consumers.

More sophisticated models began to appear. Figure 3.3 shows one created by Ian Walker, a partner at CSC, to describe how firms could collaborate through "business tubes" to connect their processing with specific market channels. In this model, suppliers would work with a firm by bringing the goods and products they needed to one or more supply chain tubes, which in turn would provide finished products for one or more markets. The processes, skills, products, and channels of distribution all became part of the subsequent improvement effort.

Chains Are Just Pieces of a Broader Network

With continued scrutiny of real processes and interactions, it became obvious that the early models were oversimplified. Most firms found

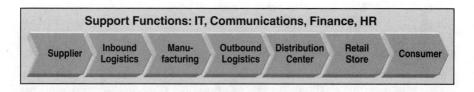

Figure 3.2 The Enlarged View of Supply Chain

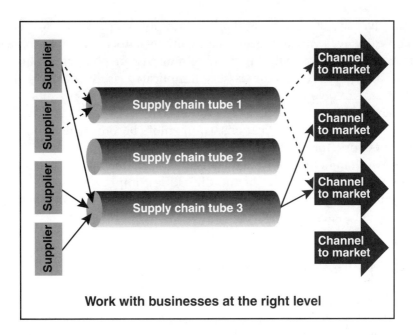

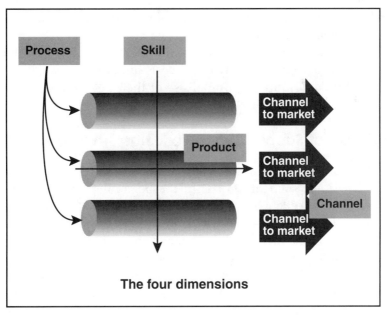

Figure 3.3 Supply Chain Collaboration Through Business Tubes (Source: Research Services Journal)

themselves involved in more than one supply chain and discovered the complexity was much greater than initially anticipated. The original pictures had to be replaced with something that involved much broader connectivity. The real picture is very complicated, as illustrated in Figure 3.4. It can involve multiple sources of supply, contract manufacturers, and several different channels to market. This larger and more complex view has significant implications; competitors become connected in the same network, forcing internal and external partners to look again at the nature of shareholder value and the network's value proposition to these shareholders. Yet in spite of the difficulties, improvement efforts can move to the highest level because every aspect of the business processing becomes subject to analysis and possible improvement.

These Pictures Apply to Other Industries

This more complex and more realistic picture is relevant well beyond the bounds of classic Porter value chain businesses like manufacturing and retail. Financial services and healthcare firms, which create value by networking with their customers, suddenly saw the importance of working across business boundaries to improve the operation of the network as a whole. Car rental organizations, hotels, and airlines now look to supply chain concepts, not only to cut costs but also to create incentives for customers and to make optimal use of their network assets.

The Scope of Supply Chain Work Has Broadened

The notion of the supply chain pushes firms into a progressive broadening of their improvement efforts. In the beginning, the focus was on manufacturing excellence within the four walls of the firm. But the supply chain idea forced them to look both upstream to suppliers and downstream to customers and seek enhancements to the whole sequence of process steps. Early efforts were focused on the neighboring links in the chain, largely because it was hard to see any further up or down the chain, but the objective is to take a much broader view and to focus on optimizing the total system of interaction, from the supplier's supplier right through to the customer's consumer.

This later view positions a firm as part of a larger "network" system and requires it to look hard at its core capabilities, its competitive advan-

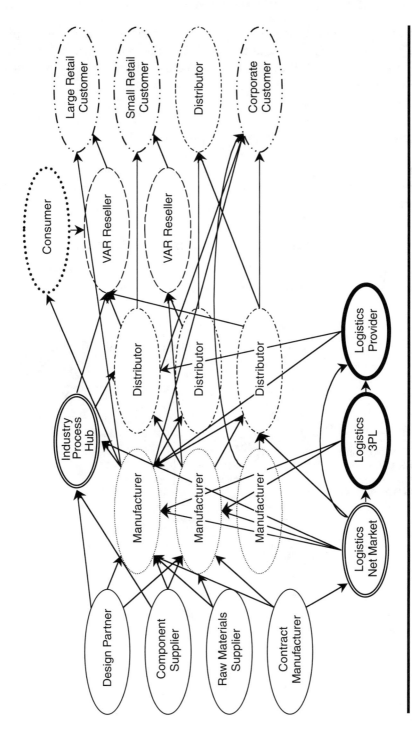

Figure 3.4   Supply Chains Are Becoming Collaborative Networks

tages, and its interenterprise relationships. Increasingly, this orientation has led managers to realize that the firm's business values are defined by the processes in which they can play a role and the value they bring to these processes.

Supply Chain Evolves Through Five Levels

Supply chain work itself evolves through five different levels with five different sets of concerns and different benefits to be gained at each stage (Figure 3.5).

Level 1 Is About Improvement of Functional Processes

In the first level of the evolution, the focus is on functional processes, as the enterprise moves toward integration of its internal best practices and

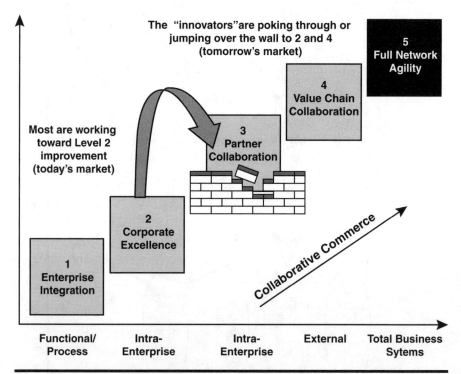

Figure 3.5   The Five Levels of Supply Chain Evolution

seeks the kind of savings that will persuade management to support the effort. There is very limited visibility across the wider supply chain, and it is difficult, for example, to respond to customer requests for information without some form of manual activity. It is also difficult to change existing processes, so there is very little flexibility in the way things are done.

At this entry level, the best features and practices of the earlier continuous improvement efforts are brought forward and merged under the supply chain umbrella. This step is very important. Many firms have tried to start with a so-called clean sheet, and they wasted all the learning from previous efforts and disappointed the people who had labored so hard to find the earlier improvements. With the best internal practices brought forward, the company then focuses on internal and functional process improvement, usually beginning with sourcing and logistics as the two areas that offer the most immediate opportunities. Teams are formed, root cause analysis is promoted as a learning tool, and efforts are launched to find the low-hanging fruit so that cost savings can be garnered and documented.

These first efforts have their successes and their difficulties. Success generally comes by leveraging volumes with a reduced supplier base to realize better price savings and later through improvements that are usually found in transportation and warehousing. The initial problems revolve around the unwillingness of the functions and business units to cooperate, even in the interests of better overall company performance. Progress is inhibited by their anxiety to maintain their autonomy and to maintain control of valuable data within their limited spheres of operation. Typical level 1 savings are in the region of 5 to 8 percent of the procurement costs and a similar 5 to 8 percent in logistics costs.

Level 2 Is About Greater Internal Cooperation

In the second level of the evolution, a firm continues to focus internally, but it begins to break down the walls between functions and business units and starts to move toward corporate optimization. This is the level at which most companies are currently working on their supply chain. The implementation begins to pick up steam at this level, and a supply chain leader is selected to direct the effort. With the support of most senior managers, particularly the chief executive officer and chief information officer, this leader works to demolish the inhibiting silos and builds some intraorganizational cooperation, often starting in areas that do not affect a business unit's market performance, such as indirect spending. Purchases across the firm are aggregated to increase the total buying leverage in specific categories, and the lower prices serve to demonstrate the benefit of broader organizational cooperation. Warehouse space is investigated to see if company benefits can be derived from better overall use, and third-party transportation and storage organizations are brought in to determine if further logistics savings can be generated.

Technology is an important enabler of this cooperation and integration. Integration technologies such as middleware, integration brokers, and enterprise application integration are deployed because without these pragmatic tools, the cost of breaking the stovepipes can jeopardize the entire supply chain effort.

With some documented savings, the effort expands. Distribution space, transportation fleets, equipment, and systems are all investigated to see if reductions can be achieved in the capital invested. Warehouse management systems and transportation management systems are implemented. Information transfer between units is encouraged and leads to the introduction of an intranet, linking the various functions and business units to valuable data.

Whole processes get a complete makeover. Engineers begin to design products that are manufacturing friendly. Order entry and management are standardized, and errors in such processing are more or less abolished. Planning moves from an MRP or MRP II system to sales and operations planning and, further, to an advanced planning and scheduling format. Inventory management becomes a serious effort, and some savings are shown in working capital, mostly through simple transfer of ownership. Annual carrying costs are lowered as a consequence for a firm moving the inventories to an obliging supplier.

The best systems begin to provide visibility of the total inventories across the system, matched with manufacturing and delivery capacity, so that a firm can define the capacity it has available to fill orders (capable-to-promise) or tell a customer what it can deliver from its inventory and when (available-to-promise). A typical level 2 firm will add two to three points of net profit to its bottom line.

Level 3 Requires a Cultural Shift — And a New Technology

Most firms pursuing supply chain improvement get bogged down in level 2. The program stalls as further internal efforts reap diminishing returns. Reaching the third level of supply chain evolution requires vaulting over a significant cultural and technical wall. The key characteristic of level 3 is that the scope of improvement work expands to include multiple companies, which work in concert to improve both internal and external processing for the benefit of the customer. Designing processes from the perspective of the customer has become something of a mantra, but it presents a considerable challenge. New processes must be designed from the top down, in line with a firm's objectives and understanding of customer requirements.

Indeed, the ultimate process model must extend across the disparate legacy systems of the business partners so they can collaborate to serve their customers and end consumers. There is widespread acknowledgment that supply chain processes run across several businesses, but they are rarely defined explicitly. Business relationships are conventionally defined by deliverables at the points of interface and they share information by messaging technology (electronic data interchange and e-mail) and by publishing data at the same interface points through supplier and customer portals.

Most managers are happy to live on their islands, and conventional thinking inhibits the use of external resources for anything other than finding further cost reductions for the firm itself. The internal organization may be keen to acquire external information because it might be valuable to the firm, but it will not give up any internal data to anyone else. Good ideas must be presented as having originated from internal sources, and the need for external advice is a mark of ineptitude. These building blocks of the restraining wall are cemented together with ignorance about the technological enablers of information sharing between business allies.

Typically, one business unit breaks out of this cultural straightjacket under the direction of a visionary leader who enlists the help of the supply chain leader, the chief information officer, and chief procurement officer and begins partnering with a few carefully selected business allies. An interenterprise effort is launched, and the need for technical assistance quickly becomes apparent.

BUSINESS PROCESS MANAGEMENT SOLVES THE TECHNOLOGY PROBLEM...

The parochial nature of conventional thinking and the job structures and measurement schemes that reinforce it are formidable obstacles to collaboration between companies. In fact, they are usually cited as the

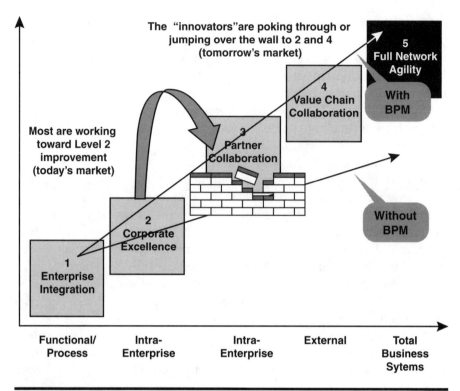

Figure 3.6 Improving Supply Chain Evolution with BPM

major barriers to change at this level of the supply chain evolution. But the truth is that even if everyone understood the message, everyone was convinced, and everyone was eager to collaborate, they could still be deterred by the immense technical barriers that have never been eliminated. Real processes run right across organizational boundaries, and they require the integration of hundreds of systems running on dozens of different technology platforms. Up to now, this level of integration has required the acceptance of a common technology standard — and virtually every attempt to do that has been overwhelmed by new waves of innovation.

Business process management (BPM) technology, as shown in Figure 3.6, puts a new layer into the architecture, allowing businesses to implement shared processes without having to change their underlying technology investments or even having to agree on a common messaging standard to access them. All they really have to do is agree on a common high-level language such as Business Process Modeling Language to express the business process at the highest level. Once they have defined the overall process, they can agree on how it is to be divided up and define the processing interfaces, the points where they will exchange information and hand control from one firm to another. The BPM engines will then manage all the required exchanges.

...AND THE NETWORK BEGINS TO FUNCTION

The elements of external collaboration can then be seeded, usually through a pilot experiment, and network formation can get under way. Procter & Gamble and Wal-Mart are poster children in this area. Their relationship stands out as an example of what can be accomplished when collaboration is used to extend a supply chain effort. For more than seven years, these two proud and powerful firms have been working together to share best practices and create one of the most effective supply chain networks in the consumer goods and retailing markets.

Under their redesigned system, the stockkeeping units were whittled down to what Wal-Mart stores needed from P&G as the supplier. P&G took over replenishment deliveries and stocking of its products through its vendor-managed inventory system. It receives data from the cash registers daily, matched with a 52-week planning forecast, which is adjusted for actual conditions. Data are shared on consumer buying patterns so that offerings can be matched to local demand, and promotions are planned and executed on a joint basis so that the increased demand can be predicted and monitored.

Level 4 Is Where Partners Look
for Growth Opportunities Together

The next step is to the fourth level: value chain collaboration. Now the external environment is fully understood and a drive is under way to create supply chain visibility. BPM is at full throttle, and allies are applying electronic commerce, activity-based costing, and balanced scorecards to root out all of the extraneous costs and nonvalue-adding process steps. True external collaboration is thriving, and the focus moves to the end consumer and how the linked partners in the network can collaborate to build new revenues. The attention to cost reduction never goes away, but the relative emphasis moves to the top line of the profit-and-loss statement and how to generate new sales that benefit all parties in the extended enterprise. Synchronization across this enterprise becomes a shared goal, and sharing of talent becomes a viable proposition.

Boeing offers a fine example of the benefits of such an advanced position. The 777 airplane was designed in virtual cyberspace and came to market in record time. Boeing worked its entire network into the project, including engineers, key airline customers, major component suppliers, project managers, and maintenance personnel, to make sure the new model met or exceeded customer and quality needs. The design was interactive and there were no paper blueprints. Communication and data transfer were handled over the Boeing extranet, linking its global partners. The typical 3-year delivery time was cut to 8 to 12 months through this collaborative effort.

Technology is a key factor in enabling this level of collaboration. Order entry, interactive planning, inventory management and control, and a host of other activities that used to be handled on an individual firm basis are under the microscope to determine how total value chain solutions can be found that help all the parties. But the solutions available up to now have been so expensive, so rigid, and so time consuming to deploy that very few networks — even with the drive from a committed nucleus firm — ever managed to get to this level of evolution.

Level 5 Is Rarified Space

Level 5 is as much conceptual as it is factual. It is the objective of level 4 initiatives and the goal of the whole supply chain effort. It is "supply chain nirvana." The idea is to develop the electronic links between the collaborating firms to the point where *full network connectivity* is achieved. This produces a shared total business system, which provides on-line visibility across the entire network of all inventory and shipments. Cycle time from new product design to commercial acceptance is at unprecedented low levels, and the rate of success with such new introductions rises dramatically. BPM technology becomes the enabling factor as the linked firms move toward optimization of the whole business network.

The Steps Must Be Followed, But the Results Can Be Significant

In spite of the potential, the current focus of most supply chain efforts remains on the acquisition and movement of goods and the optimization of internal processing. It will require time, patience, the honing of skills, and, most likely, more success stories to impel organizations to the advanced levels being considered here.

Supply chain improvement is incremental. The levels of the evolution cannot be skipped, and a firm must find its way through each level and polish its ability to collaborate and to apply technology successfully. The links will get better, first internally and then externally with a limited number of supply chain partners. Trust becomes the adhesive ingredient that really facilitates network formation and expansion, and BPM makes a technical solution feasible without having to bet the whole business. Pilots and experimentation build greater trust as the partners learn what they can and will share effectively. With greater trust comes the success that drives the effort forward still further.

Experience with many firms in many different industries shows the kind of benefits that can be achieved. These include:

- Shorter lead times and cycles, often reduced by as much as 40 to 50 percent
- Better, more accurate order entry and tracking, requiring far less reconciliation
- On-line visibility of raw materials, work in process, and finished goods across the total network, with the ability to divert in transit, if necessary
- Less need for inventory and safety stocks, often allowing reductions of 40 to 50 percent
- Use of virtual logistics methods to cut transportation costs by up to 10 percent
- Building of new revenues, often in nontraditional areas, by as much as 5 to 10 percent
- Reduction of general, selling, and administrative costs in the range of 5 to 10 percent

These benefits translate directly into profits. When CSC conducted a study of leading firms to determine the level of savings that could be generated from an intense supply chain effort, the results were impressive. As shown in Figure 3.7, results in each area varied widely, but the overall conclusion is that the new opportunities can bring a total of six to eight points of additional profit to a firm.

Inventory reduction alone, by means of ridding the network of excess safety stocks and having the right amount of the right product at the point of need, can increase profits by 1 to 2 percent. Reduced logistics costs can provide another 1 percent, while efficiencies in direct and indirect spending might add over 2 percent. Total supply chain cost

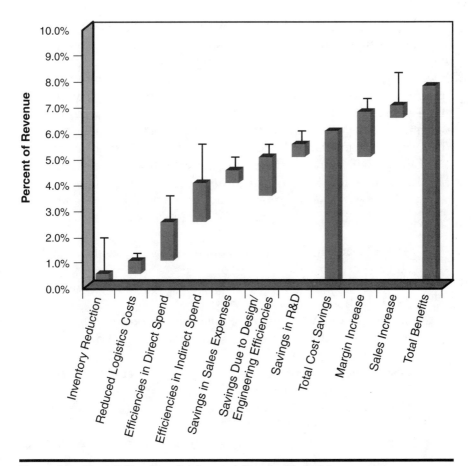

Figure 3.7 Overall Benefits of Advanced Supply Chain Management

savings can reach 6 percent, and, as Figure 3.7 indicates, another 2 points can be derived from working with supply chain constituents to raise prices (for superior products and services to the customer) and build new revenues.

BPM Provides Other Benefits That Will Make It Very Hard to Resist

So far, we have introduced BPM technology only as the key to integrating all the hundreds of systems that dozens of supply chain partners will be using without having to agree on a common technology base. But it has a number of other selling points, which among them make it a very attractive and practical proposition for almost any enterprise.

- BPM is extremely useful internally, to solve smaller scale problems at levels 1 and 2. At level 1, it can be used to refine internal processes without having to modify the applications and packages that drive them. By taking control of the process logic from the outside, it allows a firm to define a new and much more flexible process while still using the original system to do the processing. (The Tesoro case, to be discussed later, illustrates the potential in this area.)

  At level 2, BPM can be used to integrate internal systems to remove manual steps, to reduce time and to eliminate errors — and it can do so much more cheaply, more quickly, and more flexibly than other technologies. (The Iowa Telecom case will describe this opportunity.)

  The result is that by the time businesses want to push on to level 3, and start serious external collaborations, many firms will already have the key technology in their arsenal.

- BPM will appeal to smaller companies because it comes in at a price point that makes it accessible to them and makes it possible for them to participate in multiple networks. It will be easy to define variant process models for multiple customers and suppliers, to implement them quickly, to manage them as data items in a repository, and to apply them to the right transactions.

- BPM solves the "agreement problem" by creating "zones" within which a single partner can take responsibility for the processing details. It cuts through the Gordian knot that stifles almost every current attempt at collaboration: businesses cannot reach agreement on every detail of the way they will work together and are fearful of being bound by such agreements even if they could concur.

  BPM is designed to ensure that they do not have to comply with these limitations. Partners do not have to agree on the whole detailed process map and they do not have to improve it all at once or in one spectacular implementation. What they must do is agree on a common high-level model — a so-called "public process" that serves as the integration platform. Then, if they choose, each firm can take sole responsibility for the details of its own area, creating "private processes" that give it full control of its own work as long as it fulfills the commitments to other parties defined in the public process. The parties can get something working first and then begin to improve it collaboratively later, once they have the benefit of the visibility and flexibility that BPM provides.

■ "Private processes" can also be used to protect commercially sensitive information. Firms can either keep processes secret if they believe there is a competitive advantage that needs protection, or, if it is more beneficial, they can use the process engine to provide trusted partners with real-time access to a portion of their internal operations. In the near future, as this practice gains momentum, we expect to see businesses succeeding in making themselves partners of choice, not so much because they have brilliant process designs but because they are able to provide visibility and control to network partners and key customers.

Conclusions

As supply chain continues to be an improvement technique for more and more companies, and firms discover their way through the various levels of the evolution, several factors will become apparent:

1. The leaders are well out in front, but there are so few of them that, for all intents and purposes, the advanced areas of supply chain management present a level playing field.

2. It takes a sustained network effort to make up the ground. It requires a high level of commitment to beyond internal improvements, to partner with a few key allies and to begin to spell out how to get to the desired future level of accomplishment and how to share the benefits.

3. Using BPM as the next enabler can propel a firm and its allies forward at a very fast pace. The reward can be dominance in a particular industry or market segment.

4. A level 5 business would live in the world of co-managed value chains. It would be collaborating with many firms, probably in several networks, and indeed doing so legally with some of its competitors for the purpose of meeting market needs. It would have mapped its processes explicitly and linked them to its information technology infrastructure using process technologies. It

would maintain the process models as intellectual capital and would understand deeply how they relate to those of competitors, creating actionable knowledge from which to plan its business operations, week to week, quarter to quarter, and year to year. From this elevated process view, such a company would come to understand its true sources of shareholder value and its fundamental propositions in competing with other chains.

4

TECHNOLOGY WILL BE THE SOLUTION — AS SOON AS IT STOPS BEING THE PROBLEM

In moving beyond level 2 and starting to collaborate seriously with supply chain partners, a business is presenting itself with a number of increasingly complex and difficult challenges. Technology will clearly be a part of the solution, but so far its track record has not been very good. It has not even been good at responding to the challenges of levels 1 and 2, the improvement of local processes and the cross-functional integration of the firm itself. Given the stalled position of most efforts, business process management (BPM) technology is arriving just in time.

The Business Environment Is Becoming More and More Challenging

The challenges of improving the supply chain are not self-imposed; firms are being forced to respond to a business environment that has become a lot less benevolent in the last few years. After a period of extended business prosperity, companies around the world are now facing the kind of market and economic conditions and pressures that force a greater need for performance improvement.

The major pressures come from three sources:

- **Customers**, who are becoming ever-more demanding: Whether they are business customers or end consumers, they expect high-quality products and services. They demand innovation and something that is significantly better than last year's offering. And spurred by the typical advertising and promotion that surround goods and services, they expect to get these commodities at rock-bottom prices.

  There is also a growing awareness that they can have these products and services customized to their needs:

  - Cars and personal computers are now built to customer specifications. Consumers expect to choose engine size and hard-disk capacity, and they have little patience with the supplier handling the details of the necessary logistics if the process breaks down.
  - Financial services are tailored and combined into packages that serve the needs of an individual customer. Suppliers are expected to know the business and markets well enough to help provide individual solutions and to assure the required legal backing.
  - Suppliers are being expected to take on more responsibility for the operation of their products. The U.S. Navy already has suppliers on board its ships assisting with new and complicated technology advances in weaponry and guidance.

  These conditions can turn a product into a service, and they result in suppliers taking over part of the customer's business processing. Pratt & Whitney and Rolls Royce won't sell an aircraft engine; they will provide Boeing and Lockheed with power by the hour. PPG won't sell paint to carmakers; it will assume responsibility for painting cars on the production line. Pharmaceutical firms won't sell insulin; they will provide information and tools for patients to manage their condition.

- **Competitors**, who are altering their traditional positions: Suppliers of products and services are not only serving their own customers well, they are stealing them from each other. And these customers/consumers tend to show little loyalty. They regard it as their right to be able to move between suppliers, even if what they bought involved substantial investment and development and is highly customized to their requirements.

Even more troubling, new competitors — businesses like banks, insurance companies, and logistics providers that were once thought of as mere enablers — are marching into other people's markets with strong brands and new service offerings. Their threat is not that they can replace the whole supply chain, but that they can pick off the pieces of it that actually make the money. Insurance companies in particular are into this tactic as they try to offer a full range of financial services to their clientele.

To keep their own customers and to steal others, businesses have become outstandingly effective, efficient, and user friendly. They are responding to competitive pressure in a number of ways:

☐ Firms are looking at their own internal operations from the customer's point of view, eliminating work that adds no value and finding opportunities to provide more value and convenience in ever-shorter time frames.

☐ They are finding ways to extend this logic to the whole supply chain and find additional savings that could come from atypical alliances. They are using technology to collaborate with their first- and second-tier suppliers and other business partners to drive costs out of the supply chain and to increase customer satisfaction.

☐ They are extending this collaboration idea by shedding inefficient and ineffective components of their business and finding partners that can do things better. Often the lack of efficiency is overcome by outsourcing some of the process steps to a competitor.

Sorting through these alterations to determine the effect on normal business roles is forcing companies to rethink their markets and industries as they develop their advanced supply chain efforts.

■ **Change** and meeting new challenges: Businesses have always had to worry about market changes and making appropriate responses, but today it is more like responding to a constant deluge of complications. There is more need for change than ever, at a more rapid pace — and nobody expects things to get any slower. Changes in technology make more things possible, and that creates new expectations, new buying habits, and new demands. Just when consumer products companies and retailers had generation X figured out, along come generations Y and Z — groups that believe their human rights are violated if information is not instantly available to them.

At the same time, open borders and new forms of communication are opening markets and exposing customers to new products and services and new suppliers. Global commerce can increase market penetration, and even small firms expect to reach customers all over the world. All of this pressure for change is creating financial demands as turnover and profit margins are threatened in the quest to maintain pace.

In summary, the pressures for change are forcing a firm to move its supply chain effort beyond any stalled position at level 2 and accelerate the progression to level 3 and higher with help from willing allies — or become the victim of more agile, networked competitors.

Businesses Must Respond with a New Wave of Process Work

These challenges are unprecedented, but there are lesson to be learned from previous improvement initiatives. One of the earlier responses to these types of pressures came through business process reengineering (BPR), which promised to increase effectiveness and reduce costs without requiring lots of up-front cash. What it did require was an investment in time and effort. It was cheap and low risk, and if you could do it right, the rewards would be large. That same recipe would have immediate appeal in the face of today's conditions — if the key ingredients were available.

The original recipe for BPR was simple: look at the processes involved in a business function from end to end and then eliminate what is unnecessary, automate what is routine, and empower people to add value at the points where they really should make an impact. The recipe this time is not much different, except that the focus has shifted to the bits we couldn't improve the last time around — the problems that were too hard to resolve and the areas that were out of reach of the process designers. In particular, we now have to confront the issues that are outside the control of the individual businesses and which require collaboration between them.

This deeper effort begins with eliminating as much of the nonvalue-adding processing work as possible. The first step is to break down the organizational stovepipes that partition work into separate channels, so the process can be viewed and understood as a whole. Last time it was the functional stovepipes that had to be demolished; this time, it is the company boundaries themselves that must be challenged. That is the only way a firm moves out of a stalled position and progresses into a networked environment. As businesses then begin to move into the external domain, and start collaborating to deliver greater value, they will discover the necessity to improve the processes that are shared across companies, which must be analyzed, understood, and made more customer focused.

The second step is to automate routine work. For many firms, much of the small-scale automation work is already done, as many of the local process fragments have been automated by software applications. But when the focus is switched to the larger scale processes, such as advanced planning and scheduling (APS), supplier relationship management (SRM), customer relationship management (CRM), collaborative planning, forecasting, and replenishment (CPFR), and a host of e-business solutions, these applications become part of the problem. Automating bigger processes across business boundaries will involve integrating their applications, something they were never designed to facilitate. The existing fragments can only be integrated into a larger automated process if a new system is introduced, something that will guide the whole process to a better state and drive the existing applications using explicit and flexible rules. No such system existed before BPM.

The third step is to empower people to add value. The valuable lessons from BPR are often forgotten in this area. Eliminating unnecessary work and automating routine work are both ways of reducing the need for people and gaining new efficiencies, but some management teams were so focused on cost cutting that their imagination went no further. The result is that process improvement work has gained a reputation for being disempowering and antipeople, reducing them to the role of mere workflow slaves, if they have a role at all.

But businesses cannot be fully automated. People are crucial to the whole enterprise, and their contribution must be made as valuable as possible. Process work can and should empower people in three ways:

- Process work empowers people by giving them visibility and some level of control over the way the business actually works. Once the business is mapped, it becomes comprehensible, and when people understand what is happening, both correctly and incorrectly, they can redesign it. Of course, in the first wave of BPR this mapping was only local, within the borders of a single company, and control was limited to a single redesign project. Unfortunately, there was no way of building the new process into the business systems and the process maps tended to languish in cupboards and rapidly become out of date.

■ Process work distinguishes the decision-making and problem-solving tasks — where people are vital — from the routine tasks that can and should be automated. Clearing away the clutter of routine administration leaves knowledge workers free to concentrate on the important aspects of their work, making them more valuable, more satisfied, and maybe even better paid as a result.

■ Process work reveals the big business picture, the end-to-end perspective that exposes the areas in which creative people should be collaborating to address a whole problem rather than trying to solve different pieces of it in isolation. Different departments (that is, different disciplines) often apply their expertise and creative energies to a problem as they see it, without fully appreciating that they see only one part of the elephant. The structural engineer, the stylist, and the manufacturing engineer are all engaged in creating a car that works, looks good, and can be built economically, but they cannot do the job separately. Working as a team, they are not only more efficient but are capable of coming up with more innovative solutions.

So businesses can address their current challenges with a new wave of process work, but this presents a raft of new challenges for information technology (IT), which we have noted is ill equipped to respond and is often regarded as part of the problem.

Advanced Supply Chain Initiatives Require a Strategic Approach

Collaborative process design is too complex and too important to be approached in an ad-hoc way. It must be approached strategically with the commitment and sponsorship of all the participating parties. Supply chain interactions have become too complex and too dependent on digital communication to be handled in separate pieces. Business allies cannot leave it to chance that they will happen to find the best practices at each point of handoff. The puzzle has to be put together through interenterprise collaboration, application of the right technologies, and finding the end-to-end solutions that differentiate the network in the eyes of the intended consumer group. Such solutions often go well beyond existing "best practices."

Process design begins with agreement on, and alignment of, the fundamental strategies that are going to be applied to a customer or customer segment. Value, products, and services are no longer dictated by the nucleus firm but negotiated directly with the customer. Once the value proposition is defined, a fulfillment process is designed and deployed. That can be done centrally by a nucleus firm and extended later with the help of business allies, or it can be co-developed with business partners.

Analysis and redesign then continue through the functions listed in Figure 4.1. Typically, a firm and its allies move from lower level (1 and 2) supply chain processing, such as procurement and logistics improvement, through mid-level processing (3 and above), including demand management, capacity planning, and sales and operations planning. As skills are gained and collaboration expanded, the network partners move further into the advanced levels (4 and above), which include APS, SRM, CRM, collaborative design and manufacturing, and CPFR.

Implementation usually begins with a few strategic suppliers that can make a real difference to the product and service offerings, to complete their work on sourcing, logistics, scheduling data transfer, and inventory control (the level 2 work) and then move on to define innovative features that could distinguish what the enterprise as a whole brings to the market. Enterprise applications are reviewed with these suppliers, strategies discussed, planning information shared, and deliveries matched better with capabilities and actual customer demand. The joint efforts are focused first on key business customers and then the end consumers.

Business customers typically enter the picture next, as the network expands and the framework extends to meeting the needs of those customers and their final consumers. They typically demand delivery through multiple channels of distribution (often involving distributors) and systems that can be connected so they can collaborate to reduce their need for inventory. Payment also comes under consideration so that bills can be paid quicker.

Process	Functions	Advanced Capability
Supply Chain Management End-to-End Product/Service Delivery	■ Order processing ■ Design, plan, buy, make, sell, deliver, collect	■ e-Business ■ Full network connectivity
Procurement Sourcing Material/ Service Acquisition	■ Supply base ■ Enterprise leverage ■ Strategic sourcing ■ Key suppliers	■ Auctions ■ Just-in-time scheduling ■ Network collaboration
Logistics Transportation, Storage, Delivery	■ Enterprise leverage ■ Selective outsourcing ■ Asset utilization	■ Virtual systems ■ Global tracking and delivery ■ Consortium distribution
Demand Management Forecasting, Planning, and Order Management	■ Sales forecasting ■ Order processing ■ Stockkeeping unit consolidation ■ Replenishment	■ Consumption trigger ■ Higher turns ■ High forecast accuracy ■ Low forecast bias
Capacity Planning and Inventory Management	■ Supply capability ■ Core competence ■ Cycle time consistency ■ Inventory, buffers	■ Flexible response ■ Lower variability ■ Constraint elimination
Sales and Operations Planning	■ Matching supply and planning ■ Performance review ■ Strategic use of resources	■ Value chain planning ■ Synchronized material flow ■ High service/fill rates
Advanced Planning and Scheduling	■ Manage volatility ■ Available-to-promise ■ Distribution planning	■ Balanced costs ■ Lead time reduction ■ Integrated work processing
Supplier Relationship Management	■ Key supply arrangements ■ Standards, protocols ■ e-Procurement ■ Partnering in trust	■ Network visibility ■ Revenue development ■ Vendor-managed inventory ■ Joint strategies/planning
Customer Relationship Management	■ Customer segmentation ■ Customer analytics ■ Data sharing ■ Joint business goals	■ Network market knowledge ■ Joint technology adoption ■ Database marketing

Figure 4.1   The Networked Enterprise (Source: CSC's Research Services)

Process	Functions	Advanced Capability
Collaborative Design and Manufacturing	■ Selective supplier assistance ■ Product life cycle management ■ Time to market	■ End consumer satisfaction ■ SRM/CRM convergence ■ Collaborative product design ■ Higher success rate
Collaborative Planning, Forecasting, and Replenishment	■ Channel partner cooperation ■ Technology application ■ Material/product visibility	■ Automatic replenishment ■ Joint sales forecasting ■ Action matches with variance ■ Network management

Figure 4.1 The Networked Enterprise (continued)

As the effort extends from end to end, from suppliers to consumers, all manner of issues appear, and the network is stretched to meet final needs accurately or accept the inevitable returns. This is where we come across the issues of promotions, sales events, product selection (so the right goods are ready when the market demand is at hand), service needs, and reaction to trend analysis. Consumers begin to dictate the requirements for the new business model that emerges, solutions are provided that differentiate the network from alternatives, and the parties start to look for mutual benefit rather than pursuing their own interests.

As you study the framework, consider where your firm fits currently and which of the many elements arrayed in the various sectors are being addressed well enough to declare victory at levels 1 and 2. Then consider the need for further interaction and connection between the players, depending on the role your firm must play in moving to level 3 and beyond. Keep in mind that some firms may be a supplier to one business network and a customer in another. At all times, remember that the consumer has taken charge of much of what gets processed through the model, and satisfaction of the targeted group must become a network responsibility. Finally, take an honest look at where the tools and technology enablers are working and not working (i.e., where the points of pain in the existing system still exist).

Then attention can be turned to improvement. Best practices are fairly well understood, but it is important for businesses to focus on process management so that these practices bring the greatest return to the participants.

Customers Complicate the Picture
by Demanding Customization

To illustrate this point, consider the drive to build new revenues, which has become a key ingredient of advanced supply chain management (ASCM). As companies recognize the complexity of their business environment, and particularly the differences between their customer and consumer markets, it becomes clear that BPM is becoming more of a challenge than just introducing a single best practice. Few businesses can afford to lose an important customer, whatever their demands; hence the large number of consumer products companies with supply chain teams living in Bensonville, Arkansas, the retail epicenter and worldwide headquarters of Wal-Mart. More and more customers are demanding the same kind of special treatment, and the usual response is an ad-hoc program to meet their demands — often outside the corporate IT application infrastructure. This is expensive and builds chaos, not control.

Businesses cannot respond to this enlarging demand for customization without a change to their business model. They will have to take a more strategic approach and move from chaos to control by segmenting customers and defining the capabilities needed in the business processes that serve them and the ways these will lead to new revenues. Some of these segmentation factors may be based upon size or profitability and reflect business strategy in certain markets. For example, smaller, less profitable customers may be serviced best over the Internet or by telephone, although your ability to do this may be restricted by law or regulation. Geographic location and regulations such as health and safety laws may dictate what suppliers are used and how work is done. Another factor might be perceived consumer preferences; for example, suppliers may be chosen that are compatible with a code of conduct or brand image.

Your processes will also need to reflect the differences in strategy of your business customers. Businesses with a similar primary strategy may distinguish themselves from competitors on a secondary strategy and require very different levels and type of support. For example, Wal-Mart, Target, and General Dollar share a primary strategy of "every day low prices," but Wal-Mart promises the greatest selection of brand name products. It requires its suppliers to provide vendor-managed inventory to make sure the mix of products at each store matches the buying patterns of that store's customers. Target, on the other hand, promises high-fashion goods. Its suppliers must analyze point-of-sale information and provide just-in-time manufacturing to stock the shelves with goods that meet absolutely current demand. General Dollar promises a selection of familiar household goods ready at hand. This firm requires little high-tech inventory management and logistics, but it expects customized product pricing and packaging to meet the taste and budget of its customers.

IT Is Part of the Problem

Over the years, IT has carved out a niche for itself, a domain in which it works rather well. What it generally offers is something called an "application" — an island of information and logic that serves one particular purpose for one particular part of the business. There are a number of important criticisms that can be made of this approach, with the fragmentation issue being the most familiar, but the issue we want to address first is that applications serve only a very limited portion of the business need.

Applications naturally serve business activities that are simple, stable, and local, but the new wave of process work will demand that IT comes out of this corner and supports a much wider range of possibilities. Businesses want to manage activities that are becoming more complex, more dynamic and responsive to change, and which reach right across the business and out across the whole supply chain. They want to take an external perspective rather than looking only at the pieces that happen to take place within their boundaries. They have to be more flexible in order to create more value and to serve specific customers better, but they must retain visibility and control or they will end up in complete chaos.

A key feature of the broader processes is that they will inevitably involve people and automated systems. In general, the larger the scale of the process, the greater the complexity and the more intimate the mix of human and computerized activities that will be involved. Casework in help desks, insurance companies, and public services is a prime example. Computers can provide required information, they can handle the case data, and they can check for consistency with specified rules, but the caseworker has to make the real decisions. These larger scale, complex processes are currently supported rather poorly by IT. Employees often have to wrestle with multiple, unintegrated systems and applications that were designed for other purposes. The new wave of business process work will look for new economies and new value in precisely these areas, and IT must find a way to respond by enabling such activities.

Shared processes, involving several business areas — perhaps even several businesses — concurrently, present another challenge. Perhaps the prime example is manufacturing. Business customers buy products from manufacturers that buy components from suppliers that buy parts from other suppliers that buy materials from other suppliers that start the whole thing again by buying machinery from still other suppliers. Participants can no longer see themselves as islands bounded by "goods in" on one side and "goods out" on the other. Each participant must have a stronger sense of the whole process for a number of reasons, including matters of complexity, reach, and flexibility:

- Participants need visibility of the whole supply chain. Suppliers can improve their reliability and their costs if they have a better understanding of actual demand, and they can plan production to meet this demand more precisely. At the same time, the suppliers and manufacturers can make alternative plans if they get advance warning of production problems.
- Participants can collaborate on process design. The only way to define a good process is to engage all the necessary participants in a collaborative effort to redesign the whole thing, and this applies to the end-to-end supply chain.
- Participants can collaborate on business problems. Once the process is seen as a holistic system, business problems can be understood in their entirety, and different contributors can collaborate to develop solutions as a team.

IT has not been good at supporting this level of collaboration. Applications are designed for internal use, and they are so difficult to connect that only the crudest and simplest business-to-business transactions can be handled electronically. Anything more subtle or complicated requires at some point the involvement of people who can sort things out by talking to each other.

Flexible processes compound all these problems and introduce another level of difficulty for IT. Today, businesses need to be able to change their processes at will and yet still manage them effectively. An example is logistics, which once just meant the delivery of products from one place to another. Today, it can include many other optional services such as the handling of import and export documentation, the management of the customer's inventory, and the rerouting of products even while they are in transit. With volatile markets and customers, who keep changing their minds, flexibility becomes a core competency — and one that is not supported well by IT.

It is useful to distinguish three levels of process flexibility, which call for different kinds of capability in the IT department:

- **Modifying processes**: The most basic requirement for flexibility is that even well-defined standard processes have to be modified occasionally. New rules must be incorporated, new regulations complied with, and more effective operations implemented.

- **Customizing processes**: A different level of flexibility is required if a business wants to take advantage of the fact that customers differ, by customizing its processes to serve each one. The challenge is to serve hundreds or perhaps thousands of customers without collapsing into chaos. Control replaces chaos when each customer can be assessed individually, the appropriate capabilities can be assembled easily, and the resulting process can be managed effectively.

- **Driving processes**: Even the ability to customize processes is no longer sufficient. We don't expect to customize a car every time we want to travel to a new destination, and the new business environment means that businesses have to respond instantly to new requirements and change their processes in real time. What companies really need is a steering wheel from which the business processes (and indeed the business) can be driven.

IT has been bad at supporting processes that are complex or shared or which call for any significant degree of flexibility. Yet this is precisely the challenge that advanced supply chain initiatives are now presenting them with.

Previous Technology Approaches Will Not Do the Job

The challenge facing a business and its IT group, as they approach a meaningful solution to this dilemma, is essentially one of integration. In most businesses, thousands of applications, each an island of automation, sit on disparate technology platforms linked by a tangle of ad-hoc connections. Even simple customer requirements require real-time access to several unaligned and uncoordinated systems. Somehow, these applications must be knitted together into something that will support a well-understood and well-mapped enterprise effort. But the integration generally costs too much and takes too long. The last wave of process reengineering generated a deluge of requests which IT departments were hard-pressed to meet. As organizations struggled to find solutions, senior management began to appreciate the importance of IT — if only because it was often the chief obstacle to what they wanted to accomplish.

Many solutions to this problem have been tried over the years:

- Databases separated out the data from application code in the hope that a business could create a single, integrated set of data and then sit all its logic on top of it. What happened in practice was that systems developers adopted the database as a tool for making better applications. The result was that every new application built, and each new package bought, introduced a new database with a new schema of incompatible data structures and a new set of translation headaches.

- Enterprise resource planning (ERP) systems replaced swathes of older applications with a single set of logic and data that was preintegrated, at the factory. The processes were also largely predefined, but businesses often saw this as an advantage in the early stages. It is much easier to unify a company's processes because SAP requires it (especially if you can sell it as industry best practice) than to arrive at a consensus from scratch. But the lack of flexibility to meet changes in business requirements became a significant disadvantage later.

  ERP systems also introduced a new integration problem. Companies were supposed to have just one ERP system, but they somehow ended up with several, and it is not uncommon now to have dozens of them. (In fact, we encountered one large firm operating with 53 ERP systems!) Integrating these internal systems is extraordinarily hard, if not completely impossible, even when they are just different installations of the same package, and now we have the problem of integrating them across a whole supply chain. They were not designed to do that job.

- Workflow introduced a new kind of IT support for managing routine manual processes that moved paper documents among people and organizations, but it did not help people to access IT systems, let alone to integrate systems so that people got the information they needed in the form they needed it. It also provided rather poor support for the really valuable human tasks of sense making, innovation, and collaboration. Workflow tended to separate manual processes from computer processes, but it only supported the areas in which they should have been integrated.

Integration of island applications is so expensive, so time consuming, and so rigid once it is done that it is often easier to leave human beings to do the dirty work. They tend to resent being treated as automatons and they are very prone to errors, but at least they are cheap and flexible. The great irony is that this kind of "swivel chair integration" accounts for much of the wasted, nonvalue-added activity that should be removed by a process improvement initiative. IT is actually introducing useless work. If we had a smarter way of integrating applications (especially across business boundaries), then a whole raft of human activities would instantly be eliminated.

BPM Finally Allows IT to Support Complex, Shared, Flexible Processes

BPM technology solves all these technical problems by approaching them from a different angle.

- BPM systems include a comprehensive set of standard connectors for integrating modern commercial packages and a tool kit for creating connections to older systems and bespoke applications.
- They are capable of communicating with systems that use a wide variety of infrastructural protocols and messaging standards. They will connect very easily to existing middleware — and thus to all the systems already plugged into it.
- They include the capability to communicate with human beings and computer systems and to integrate their contributions in complex and sophisticated ways.
- They do not require the development of new code for each new application but integrate and coordinate other systems within the network to cope with the complexity of end-to-end processing.

  BPM systems take advantage of the trend toward *componentization* in the construction of modern applications to make the

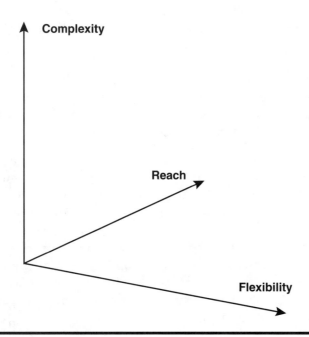

Figure 4.2 Complex Processes Have Outgrown the Capabilities of Applications (Source: CSC's Research Services)

    components interact in new ways, introducing a level of flexibility that was probably never envisaged when they were built.

■ They include a process engine, which does much more than just connect systems together and pass messages between them. It takes control of the whole environment and orchestrates the different contributions of the different systems.

■ At the heart of the BPM system is an executable, nonpolitical, business process model that a company and its IT group create together and which they use with selected supply chain partners. This model, in the form of a machine-readable language like Business Process Modeling Language, serves as the script for the process engine. The business process that used to be hard coded into the applications is now handled as data in a repository, making it very easy to introduce modifications and variants and to do so in a well-managed way.

■ They include modeling and simulation tools, which allow mixed teams of business and IT people to develop process models in a visual format and test them thoroughly before they are deployed.

- BPM systems have the built-in capability to communicate with each other and to share the management of a single process. In effect, they hide most of the complexity of shared processes.

This approach brings new and improved levels of visibility and control — central elements of ASCM, and provides vital aids in developing the external communications that become part of the networked effort. Now a firm can answer questions like: Where is my order? Where is my claim? When will I be paid? Will the parts be delivered tomorrow? Can the key suppliers have the subassemblies ready in time to fill my large order? Is my plan in sync with what is happening in the market?

With the advent of BPM, technology becomes part of the solution and helps to propel a firm and its allies beyond level 2 into the realm of ASCM. Adoption of BPM will be the catalyst that facilitates these elements and helps the business allies reap the benefits from the effort. It becomes clear that a nucleus firm can define the usable systems and move a network to level 4 and higher. Small to medium-size firms can also participate in several networks, either as a viable node on the nucleus firm's exterior network or as a partner with other firms of a similar size.

Conclusions: Managing an Advanced Supply Chain Requires a New Technology — BPM

The solution to each of the business issues we have cited comes not from applying some kind of vanilla best practice but from applying the right process for each customer and each business situation. BPM enables this kind of flexibility by avoiding the need to tweak each application and to dismantle and reassemble the enabling technology at each point of information transfer. The reduction in the lag between management intent and execution comes from responding to the business situation by means of a directly executable business model, not a self-contained and rigid off-the-shelf application. BPM represents a breakthrough in a firm's ability to manage the work of its people, systems, and organizations while leveraging the existing IT infrastructure, especially the ERP systems, thus making it possible to respond to market conditions quickly and accurately.

In this chapter, we have presented a framework for understanding how BPM and ASCM come together to ease the movement to level 3 and beyond and how to overcome the typical disparity between what a firm wants from its IT group and what it thinks it receives. In the following chapter, we will consider in more detail how BPM performs the magic that this implies.

5

DRIVE BUSINESS VALUE THROUGH PROCESS EXECUTION: SPEED, QUALITY, FLEXIBILITY, CUSTOMIZATION, AND COST

Until now, networked supply chains were possible solely for nucleus firms, or large channel masters, and their suppliers — organizations that were large enough to stand the expense of the transformation and able to agree on standard technologies. Now, a business can build networks in much shorter time frames and at greatly reduced cost, thanks to business process management (BPM) and two other trends in modern information technology (IT): componentized architectures and modern data modeling and integration tools. These three advancements allow firms to connect their businesses together into a process web by agreeing on common standards, to be used for describing business processes, thus enabling the sharing of vital information among constituents. The result is the ability for any firm in any industry to participate in a business network with superior characteristics: time to market, quality of products and services, lowest total cost of ownership, flawless order fulfillment, effective inventory management, and so forth.

These deliverables come without the high cost or time needed to build networks based on traditional technologies. Further, because the process model, and not the underlying IT applications, drives the improvements, changing the business process is as fast and as easy as changing the model. Now, a firm can pick up the need to respond to relentless demands from the customer, react better to the fierce competitive conditions, and manage the need to deliver innovative products and services in the shortest time and with the greatest flexibility. From a short-term perspective, advancing to level 3 and higher in the supply chain evolution, through creation of network value propositions, becomes possible by taking advantage of the flexibility and speed that come with BPM-oriented processing. The goal changes from finding a single best practice that aids one member of the supply chain to how the network partners collectively develop a customized solution for each customer or consumer segment, which differentiates the supplying network. The effort can then move comfortably across the end-to-end processing with the kind of visibility and control that have been sought.

In this chapter, we will explain how BPM works its magic in powering the networked supply chains of the future into advanced levels of achievement. Details of the integration features will be discussed, and the possibilities for adoption of a business process management system (BPMS) as the new engine for the supply chain effort will be presented. In a step-by-step manner, the discussion will lead to understanding that BPM is more than a breakthrough. It becomes the business solution sought by those firms determined to actively and successfully participate in the networked enterprises of the future. That accomplishment begins with knowing what the new tool is all about.

Execution Begins with Knowing What BPMS Is and Is Not

In the first place, a BPMS is not enterprise resource planning (ERP), because BPMS creates an executable process model that spans both application and organization boundaries. ERP will certainly enhance the planning and scheduling that take place inside an enterprise. It does little to facilitate the kind of cross-enterprise communication necessary for network formation. BPMS is not enterprise application integration or even business-to-business technology, because it does more than just integrate disparate systems so they can communicate together. It provides support for complex people-based activities and also enables systems integration.

On the other hand, BPMS *is* related to workflow improvement. However, it is not simply workflow technology, because it does much more than schedule work or route documents. Unlike workflow, BPMS actually does many of the complex, rules-based tasks previously assigned to people. BPMS is also not a transaction monitor, because it does more than merely track each process instance. BPMS is applied to create, execute, and optimize the business process model that powers the life cycle of each instance of the process. BPMS creates the process model and uses this model to manage the IT systems, people, and organizational infrastructure needed to execute each instance of the process.

BPM is not Web services, the name for a common framework for defining software components and invoking them using standards based on pubic Internet protocols. While BPM can manage software components that operate using Web services standards, it also works with a wide range of other methods for accessing underlying systems. This ability means BPM can perform the simple transactions supported by today's Web services standards and can handle the high-speed, secure transactions that require different types of access to IT systems.

In a business, the BPMS acts as an organizer or conductor of the whole process, keeping track of where the supply chain must get to, triggering each new stage, handling many of the exceptions that can arise when things go wrong, and putting useful control in the hands of human managers. Perhaps of greatest importance, business processes may be managed by a single BPMS or by a series of peer BPM systems, acting in concert. In essence, the key features of a BPMS are as follows.

BPMS Integrates and Orchestrates the Contributions of Other IT Systems

From one perspective, a BPMS can be thought of as smart middleware. It will connect existing communication systems together, convey the required messages from one business entity to another, and ensure that the supply chain constituents stay aligned, with the system putting all of these interactions in the context of a whole process. The system will also manage entire conversations rather than just individual messages, and it will do so from outside the systems themselves. The systems make contributions to the process, by providing data and functionality, but they are not hard-wired together. If the process script changes, so do the interactions.

A BPMS connects and integrates existing databases, legacy systems, and best-of-breed package solutions into flexible end-to-end business processes needed for advanced supply chain efforts. It increases the usefulness and value of these existing assets, and it means that new integrated systems may not be required. In fact, there could be positive value in having separate components more loosely coupled together.

BPMS Takes Advantage of the Trend in Software Componentization

Until recently, software packages were most likely to be vertically integrated and monolithic. With the advent of Java and a more object-oriented approach to systems development, software packages now have many more ways that finer grained pieces of functionally can be invoked, when and as required. The major ERP vendors are even getting on the bandwagon and beginning to provide better access to their internal modules. In an allied movement, providers of Web services are starting to invoke their own version of componentized capability. In this transition, BPM is the natural complement to component analysis and application, because it provides a disciplined way to assemble the necessary pieces to meet specific business needs.

BPMS Integrates and Orchestrates the Contributions of People

Very few business processes can or should be fully automated. Human beings add value by making judgment calls, solving problems, handling exceptions, interpreting information and learning from it, making decisions that require accountability, and forming and maintaining important business relationships with other humans. A BPMS, though, can remove much of the drudgery involved in shoveling information from one system to another system, while saving time and reducing errors in the process. However, it cannot replace human beings in the things they are really good at. A BPMS includes the ability to schedule tasks for people and to reroute them if necessary, and by using its system integration capabilities, it can present these tasks with the integrated information they need to play their part as simply and as usefully as possible.

Where such a system helps in particular is in the automation of routine and error-prone activities. The most common obstacle in this area is the "disconnect" between systems, when each one executes only part of the process. A BPMS provides a simple and flexible way to integrate such systems and to automate and optimize fragmented business processes, by providing the means to simply share required information across the users.

Allows Processes to Be Shared Across a BPMS and Across Business Boundaries

The use of a standard language for describing all aspects of a process will allow the same model to be deployed on several different systems and enable these systems to share the management of the total processing. The existence of multiple systems, such as different ERP systems, creates integration problems, especially if they come from different suppliers and reside on different technologies. A BPMS is designed to achieve the opposite effect — to establish integration capability — and is not daunted by a greater number of disparate systems. In fact, the theme becomes: the more the merrier. This capability is precisely what is required to manage distributed processes and to enable collaborative work across multiple business units and multiple business partners. A BPMS will bring all the benefits of integration, flexibility, and end-to-end visibility and control to the whole extended enterprise.

BPMS Manages Each Individual Instance of the Processes Entrusted to It

Orchestrating the contributions of systems and people means that the BPMS is responsible for the management of each instance of every process defined within it. The process model is just one design, but the process engine has to track the progress of each order, each insurance claim, each customer query, or whatever it is managing. As a side benefit, this ability provides a single point of inquiry about the state of these processes. Customers will be able to find out where their individual orders have moved to, and managers will know how their current tasks are progressing and which new ones are coming their way.

BPMS Drives Everything from the Process Model

Building a really well-integrated business process is something like building a truck; it takes a lot of effort, but if it works well, it is much more effective than a heap of parts looking for assembly. The trouble is that modifying the process can be rather like redesigning and rebuilding the truck from scratch. Building it out of Lego-like components helps, but even then it has to be dismantled and reassembled to get it to do something different.

The vision of the BPMS suppliers is that changing the process will be much more like driving the truck — doing something that the truck is designed to facilitate, just by operating the controls. The process model offers managers and process designers the controls to work with and the conversion of those control movements into swiveling of the front wheels and providing extra flows of fuel, all cared for by the BPMS. The managers and designers can just watch the road and drive the vehicle. To achieve this level of integration and flexibility in practice requires some pretty fancy capabilities. Systems must be connected and they must receive messages that they can interpret correctly. Under the covers, it is the ability to automate (or at least partially automate) the creation of connectors and the translations of meaning that really makes this feature possible.

BPMS Deploys Processes Seamlessly, Closing the Gap Between Various Management Intentions

A BPMS will allow processes to be designed on-line, by business users and process engineers together, deployed on a reliable, scalable IT infrastructure and operated thereafter by the businesses. Deployment will follow directly from process design with no intervening steps. The process model is no longer just a diagram on the wall or a set of tables in a database; rather, it is directly executable.

BPMS Records Information About the Actual Operation of the Processes

By centralizing the management of the process, the BPMS can record all information about the actual operation of every instance. Individual problems can be spotted and resolved and the pool of recorded information used to provide managers and designers with an invaluable resource for looking into opportunities to improve the process design. Keeping this information beyond the execution of the process will likely require a separate data warehouse.

BPMS Provides Feedback to the Running Processes and to the System Design

Maintenance and optimization are aided by the way that information is recorded about the execution of the process and fed back to both those in the running processes and also to those in the design function. Processes can be made to adapt automatically to business events, such as a change in the interest rate or a new sales promotion. Process design updates can be enhanced with actual performance metrics from the currently running processes.

BPMS Provides End-to-End Visibility and Control

A BPMS serves as a central point, through which processes can be conceived, deployed, optimized, and analyzed — from end to end through whatever number of people and applications are involved. The visibility that this brings to managers, the insight into the way the process should work (and the reliable information about how it really works in practice), combined with the ability to control the process and to make changes that will make things work better, means many business processes can be explicitly and effectively managed for the first time. This improvement is critically important, especially as companies begin to concentrate their efforts on what they do well and ask others to do that which they do not do well.

BPMS Supports the Needs of Different People in Different Roles

Senior managers, process engineers, departmental managers, employees, and software engineers all have a different perspective on a process and different contributions to add in making the process work effectively. A BPMS supports all these perspectives and marshals these contributions to focus all of them on the process and the value it creates.

The Magic Is Accomplished While Leveraging Existing IT investments

An extremely important feature of BPMS is that it supports a process by managing the activities of components of existing IT investments. These

IT investments can be on any IT platform and developed in any software language. They can include modern applications such as SAP, Oracle, Baan, or Siebel or a host of home-grown legacy applications and office productivity applications such as word processing and e-mail. The move is from applications to BPM.

One of the most difficult things about BPM is just explaining this feature, again in terms of what it is and what it does. At one level, BPM is a set of standards; at another, it is a set of real software products that do some fairly impressive things. However, it is difficult to grasp just what these things are because the design of the software is based upon a new idea about how different pieces of software and human activity should be integrated and coordinated. In that respect, BPM becomes the classic disruptive technology, as it challenges our core beliefs about how businesses and software should work.

In an effort to explain this new idea, let's consider a conceptual journey that begins with a conventional application and moves in four easy steps to a shared and fully BPM-enabled process. These four changes create a new kind of federated software, with a central process engine that activates and coordinates the processing.

Stage One: An Application*

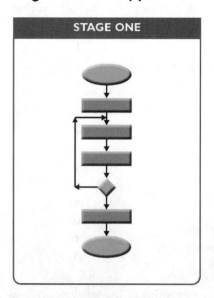

Business processes, or at least fragments of them, are conventionally managed in applications and packages. Ordering, for example, is handled by an ordering system, such as customer order management or the ordering process in an ERP package. These bundles of capability normally include business logic, rules, and data manipulation, all organized around a sequence of steps and loops that may or may not be represented very explicitly. To follow the illustration, it may be helpful to imagine an existing application in your world that you would like to enhance.

---

* Source for diagrams of the five stages is CSC's Research Services.

Stage Two: A Componentized Application

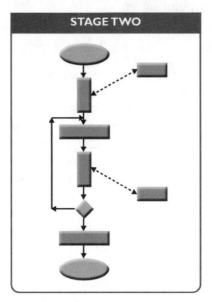

As we have discussed, an application or package may be organized into components. The main advantages of this practice are reuse and flexibility. A single component or module may be used by several different applications or packages, and it can be designed, developed, and modified freely, as long as the interface with other modules is preserved. Somewhere in the middle, however, there must be a core application that holds the logic that is unique to this particular process and which also takes responsibility for calling and coordinating the other components. Consider now the components of your application and where the critical logic resides.

Stage Three: A Naked Process

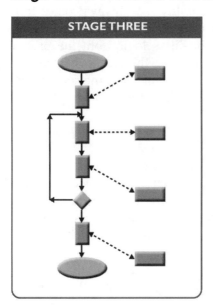

Suppose we removed everything we can from the core application — all of the business logic, all the rules, and all the data manipulation — and put them in components. What would be left? (Why we would want to do this is not yet clear, but just go with it for a while.) The irreducible responsibility of the core is to manage the logical flow, to coordinate the components, and to ensure that between them they achieve the necessary results. This requires some representation of the process, the sequence of activities, the control points, the error conditions, and the ability to handle multiple instances of such factors. An ordering system must know how the ordering process works, and it will not be of much use if it can only handle one type of order.

Stage Four: Using a Process Engine

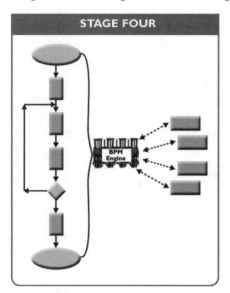

Once the core application is reduced to a naked process, then it can be defined as a script in a suitable language, such as Business Process Modeling Language, and run on a process engine that understands process concepts, knows about multiple instances, and realizes that it has to call on other components to do the real work. In fact, all applications could be reduced in the same way and all of them could be run on the same engine. Picture now that your process is broken down so that the parts you want to share are accessible by whomever you select.

The immediate advantage is the flexibility that always comes from the basic architectural principle of separating components that have different responsibilities. Separating the business logic from the process means that they can be changed independently; the process can be rearranged without having to change the components, and the components can be modified, improved, or moved to different technology platforms without impacting the overall process.

Stage Five: Sharing a Process

All of this change, however, is only doing what a conventional application can do, albeit through a better architecture and in a more flexible manner. The huge advantage comes from the ability to share the management of a process, something that is next to impossible with conventional applications and packages.

The process of ordering, for example, is not confined to the customer business. It is mirrored by the process of order fulfillment in the supplier's business. Indeed, that is one sequence of activity that is shared between

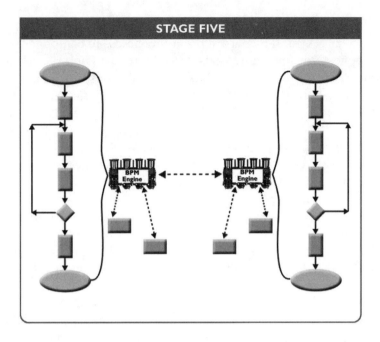

the buyer and seller, which must be carefully coordinated. The only way to make applications on both sides work effectively is to hard code them correctly. With a process definition running on a process engine, all you must do is agree on a common process. Once the process engine knows which bits are its responsibility, and which are being completed by the other business, you are up and running. Now you can link with your supply chain partners and begin improving the processing that takes place.

The Magic Also Requires Breaking Software into Components

Before you can use BPM, remember that you need to componentize your software. That is the foundation of business agility. Until recently, however, componentization was available only to those firms prepared to build their own systems or to undertake the laborious task of carving up their legacy systems at the natural joints. If a company uses packaged software, even packages based on a strong component architecture, it has little access to the underlying components.

Today, any business can componentize its software. Software vendors such as SAP and Siebel are providing access to components within their applications for two reasons. First, their customers are demanding that their applications work with other applications to support business processes that cross application and business boundaries. Second, their customers are demanding that applications be decoupled from the vendor-supplied user interfaces because they need to support business processes that cross application boundaries. These vendors have responded by providing a wide range of methods — standards-based messaging, middleware connectors, and adaptors — to access their applications and components within them.

In addition, Web services architecture is producing a proliferation of components from software vendors, which now expose their applications using Web services standards. Therefore, the packages you have invested in can be accessed through Web services standards. In addition, most software development tools now provide the tools your developers need to build new applications that can be accessed using Web services standards or to expose older applications as business services within or outside the business. The issue is not whether you should componentize your software, but rather deciding how to create and access components and the level of components that you want to access.

You can now choose to access an entire application, one subset of the application, or access a very low-level capability. For many businesses, the question is whether to use Web services standards to access their IT investments or to use middleware technology or other technologies to access the richer information of the underlying applications. Since the standards used to expose your investments have very different properties, the answer to the question will be based upon the nature of the process you want to support.

BPM Requires Capabilities Not Available from Any Single Vendor

The Business Process Management Initiative (BPMI.org), the consortium that is developing open specifications for BPM, has defined eight specific capabilities that cover all aspects of the way businesses work on their processes. These ingredients, illustrated in Figure 5.1, include:

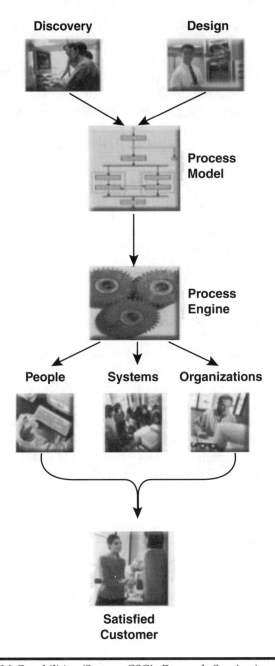

Figure 5.1   BPM Capabilities (Source: CSC's Research Services)

- **Discovery**: Capturing information about the operation of business processes (event flows, message flows, and control flows) from the perspective of all participants, including the computer systems that implement parts of the process.
- **Design**: Setting the target metrics for business processes and assembling and testing the business process components to ensure that the metrics are achieved. Processes will be assembled from components provided by your own business, by other businesses working independently, and by collaboration with them.
- **Deployment**: Rolling out new processes to all the participants involved, including people, applications, and other processes. This capability includes the automated or semi-automated creation of connections to participating systems.
- **Execution**: Ensuring that all participants (people, organizations, systems, and other processes) carry out the process. This includes the ability to identify and manage exceptions either automatically or by referring them to an expert.
- **Interaction**: Managing the interaction between the automated and manual parts of the process.
- **Operation and maintenance**: Resolving exceptions and performing other management tasks to keep the process working well.
- **Optimization**: Providing continuous feedback on the processes and suggesting alternatives to improve performance. In some cases, the optimization process may be automated and minor changes to the process may be made without human intervention.
- **Analysis**: Measuring process performance and devising improvement strategies. This is the collection, presentation, and manipulation of the analytics needed to develop new process versions.

These eight capabilities are not currently provided through products available from any single software vendor. For example, BPM vendors with strong discovery and design tools do not now have the ability to directly execute a process model. Tools that provide strong process model execution capability provide less robust discovery and design capabilities. Therefore, a firm intent on network participation must expect to build or assemble a "best-of-breed" BPM platform.

As a firm accepts this premise and begins working on the platform, it will discover that a BPMS allows it to negotiate the level of visibility and control it wants to provide to its business partners. In many cases, a business process firewall protects the security of the internal systems and the privacy of employees or customers. In essence, a BPMS mediates the connection between business partners. The operating area between the partners is the public process. The part of the process that is inside a particular partner is called the private implementation. The boundary between what is the public process and the private implementation can be adjusted dynamically according to the needs and wishes of the partners.

The BPMS is in effect a business process firewall. However, in contrast to most hardware firewalls, the configuration can be very dynamic and can change according to the needs of the business. This means that you can agree upon an explicit process with another firm and then set up the process that provides what is needed but with no visibility into your systems or information about a particular case. This condition, for example, would allow government agencies to certify to other government agencies or even third parties that citizens were eligible for benefits (healthcare, housing, education) without disclosing sensitive information such as age, race, or heath status. Similarly, two companies that agree that employees will work together on a joint project can certify that an employee has been assigned to the project without revealing sensitive personnel files.

A BPMS also provides end-to-end management capability, even when other participants do not have a BPMS. As we have indicated, BPM introduces the capability to manage processes that span three areas: systems, people, and businesses. Once the process model has been accepted, and the network participants have agreed on a business process modeling language, the model manages the complex interactions. The model communicates with the necessary components through a wide range of standards, from other business model process modeling languages to low-level middleware messages. The BPMS keeps track of every instance of a process, leaving you in control even when processes take days or months to complete. This ability to manage and track every instance of a process is why BPM orchestrates the business processes rather than simply launch transactions. With BPM, your business can quickly replicate much of the networked supply chain capabilities of the private networks maintained by such firms as Dell and Cisco. These abilities include:

- Reduce capital requirements by producing to order instead of for stock and by taking advantage of joint assets, owned by networked partners. In a network, the most capable partner operates the machinery.

- Reduce time to market by integrating processes that take new concepts and designs from the innovator's mind or drawing board to the locations where customers can make the purchase in record cycle times. In the current environment, normal cycles are cut by 50 percent or more, and the success rate escalates, as network partners share database information on what is needed, how to create it in a collaborative manner, and how to get it in front of the right customers.
- Cut inventory by using customer point-of-sale information, better demand planning, and joint trend analysis to trigger the right requests to direct production schedules.
- Cut prices and maintain profit margins by using supplier information on price and availability to reward your best customers.
- Create new revenues, often in nontraditional areas, by introducing collaborative features that appeal to new customers. With existing customers, a sales lift can be generated by having the right products available at the point of impulse or need.

Any business that has aspirations to be a channel master will soon be implementing through a BPMS. Companies simply will not be able to compete without one. Your customers are already expecting the lower prices, visibility, and control a BPMS delivers. However, other players in the supply chain — the supplier, design helpers, and enablers (credit, logistics, tariffs, etc.) — will soon also have a BPMS to manage their processes as well.

BPM will be useful for the suppliers that want to be more than commodity players in the supply chain or those that sell into several supply chins. In the past, such a business had to support multiple technologies or forego parts of its market. For example, a business that sells into the automotive, aerospace, and chemical industries has had to comply with standards for three public marketplaces and dozens of private networks. Now each business can use a single BPMS to manage its interactions with each of the supply chain partners, including the public market spaces, and have a single integrated view of all of their processes.

Supply chain enablers such as logistics firms are quickly adopting BPM. These firms have been competing based on process excellence and their capability to provide visibility and control for over 15 years. BPM reduces the cost of process management and provides them with enhanced capability to provide each of their customers with a detailed visibly into their logistics chain. Logistics companies once prided themselves on their ability to track a package and provide on-time deliveries. With BPM, these same companies can analyze manufacturing and logistics patterns and identify potential problems and propose solutions before they occur.

A Case Study Illustrates the Possibilities

Until now, supply chain integration was an intensely manual process. Business partners would agree on new supply chain processes that they expected would take the time and cost out of their supply chain. Then each company would independently begin to develop the internal processes and IT systems needed to support the new processes. Not surprisingly, the many independent efforts, at least in the first incarnation, did not yield the expected benefits. For the most part, these failures are due to weak relationships between partners, delays in implementation, and poor coordination.

When businesses begin using a common process framework and terminology and then use process management tools based upon a common process modeling language, supply chain integration becomes easier, faster, and less expensive. For example, many global companies such as Hewlett-Packard and Siemens use the Supply Chain Council's Supply Chain Operations Reference (SCOR) model* to work with their supply chain partners. SCOR provides a common reference model and vocabulary to describe supply chain operations, best practice designs, common metrics for measuring supply chain operations, and benchmarks that can be used to set goals for reengineering the supply chain and for evaluating the success of supply chain operations. Businesses using SCOR have already demonstrated that common language, metrics, and benchmarks can accelerate the development of effective and efficient supply chains.

BPM tools speed up the deployment of this process even further. For example, IDS Scheer has developed an approach to supply chain modeling that uses a common executable modeling language to enable business to agree on supply chain processes and then execute and manage them. The IDS Scheer framework for process management shown in Figure 5.2 embraces process management from strategy to ongoing

---

* Supply Chain Operations Reference Model, Overview of SCOR Version 6.0, Supply Chain Council, 2003.

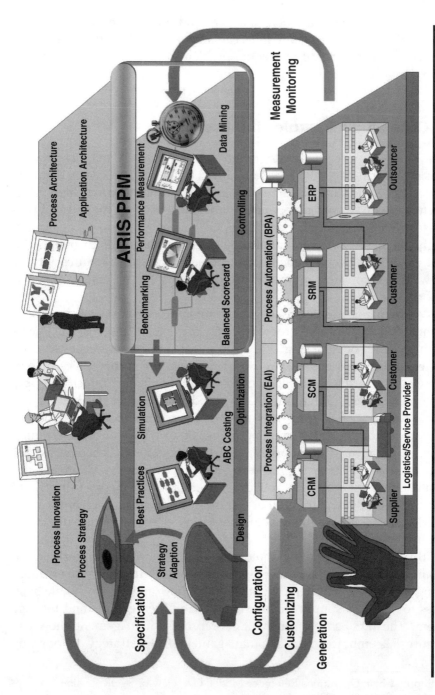

Figure 5.2 ARIS house of business process excellence (Source: IDS Scheer)

monitoring of operating processes. Customers that use this framework along with BPM tools from IDS Scheer and its partners can model supply chain processes using ARIS, IDS Scheer's modeling tool, and then use that supply chain model to execute the processes within their internal enterprise and between external enterprises.

The utility of the framework and tools is enhanced, because they are moving to a shared business process modeling language. Because IDS Scheer has close relationships with the major ERP vendors, it has developed ARIS Scout applications that businesses can use to automate what is often tedious manual processing for determining how their current process is supported by people and systems. They can then model the "to be" process and simulate the costs and benefits of the new process before deployment. Design and deployment of new processes can be done by directly configuring existing applications such as SAP and Oracle e-business suites or workflow solutions such as Staffware. BPMS such as Intalio can also execute processes modeled in ARIS. Once the processes are in operation, IDS Scheer's ARIS Process Performance Manager (ARIS PPM) can be used to measure the performance of each stage of the process and allow partners to identify points of pain. ARIS PPM is not simply a data warehouse application. Such applications provided by SAP and others are useful for financial reporting and provide some limited information on process outcomes. They do not, however, provide a useful way of monitoring processes while they are in operation or determine which activity in a complex, long-lived process is the source of friction and pain.

Loyalty Partners Uses BPM to Make Sure That Customers and Partners Are Not Lost in the Network

Loyalty Partners GmbH, based in Munich, Germany, has developed Payback — the leading loyalty card program in Germany. Over 15 million customers use its bonus card program when buying products and services from over 120 partner firms. From the customer's point of view, the loyalty card offers an easy way to earn bonus points when buying off- and on-line in a wide range of stores. Customers can then claim rewards in the form of premiums or cash awards, which are sent electronically to their bank accounts using a paper form, the telephone, or the Internet. Customers can even donate their reward points to UNICEF. From the business partner point of view, Payback provides the up-to-date records of customer purchases and rewards, allowing partner firms to track customer preferences without the cost of developing their own loyalty program. In many cases, their customers prefer the ability to build rewards across a wide range of purchases.

From the customer point of view, Payback is easy to use and provides an efficient, reliable way to access account information and to conduct transactions. The typical customer scenario runs as follows. Charles Johnson is pleased. Contrary to all expectations, he succeeded in connecting the cordless ISDN telephone he bought at a department store yesterday. However, that is not the only reason for his good mood. By buying this equipment, he saved 3 percent, which was credited to his Payback account in the form of bonus points. Because he also received points for the compass saw he purchased from a do-it-yourself firm and the detergent bought at a drugstore, his account has risen to 1510 points. He knows this by checking on the Internet — at www.payback.de. Charles can now draw out the equivalent of at least 1500 points, worth 15 Euro. To do this, he fills out a form on the Web site and sends it off. When he clicks the OK button, his request is saved in the Loyalty Partners system, along with the time and the number of his payback card.

From Loyalty Partners' point of view, that's when a complex process begins. If there is a problem at any step in the process, Charles' transaction and hundreds of similar transactions can be delayed, destroying Loyalty Partners' reputation for effectiveness and accuracy. Customers like Charles do not expect an instant response. They understand that it may take up to eight days to receive an award. This time is needed to validate that the purchaser is the legitimate bonus cardholder and to complete award transactions that may require batch processing. Charles does, however, expect that the service will be reliable and that his reward will be recorded when expected. For Loyalty Partners, the challenge is to manage the complex and long sequence of tasks and assure they are completed in the required time frame. Loyalty Partners cannot wait until the end of the time frame to discover that an error somewhere in the process has delayed Charles' reward.

Loyalty Partners' first step in process management was to model the process using IDS Scheer's ARIS modeling tool. This step enabled Loyalty Partners to have an enterprise view of its processes and to document each of the many ways a customer may interact with the company and the people, systems, and business partners participating in that process. It used those process models to develop its systems in the Oracle environment. It then used IDS Scheer's PPM to measure and manage five critical steps in the process. Loyalty Partners felt that end-to-end measurements were not enough, particularly if they came at the end of a reporting cycle. The PPM product allowed Loyalty Partners to continually measure the operation of critical steps in the process and to identify and then resolve problems before they impacted customers. Loyalty Partners was also able to generate reports that compared processes, such as differences in performance between the telephone- and the Web-based version of the same process. Customer and employee information was kept anonymous, to protect privacy. The goal was process improvement, not holding individuals accountable for problems.

The initial PPM applications were completed in less than four months by three people, two of whom were Loyalty Partners employees. Total costs were in the low six-figure range. Martin Hermann, who is responsible for quality improvement at Loyalty Partners, feels that the investment was justified by the results of the project. He claims there were no conditions to compute a return on investment. "Nevertheless," he said, "it is important to avoid costs by ensuring quality and satisfying customers. But this item cannot be quantified." PPM lets Loyalty Partners find and correct problems before they affect its customers.

Loyalty Partners is now extending the application of the IDS Scheer tool set to its programs for partners. For example, it now uses the software to manage the processing of bulk data from the partners that record the transactions from customer accounts. The next step will be to develop a process monitor of systems used to notify customers by SMS of new events or promotions such as the ability to use the card with new partners or when a customer's awards have reached a specific level, such as 1500 points.

Conclusions

With BPM, networked enterprises can proliferate, introducing a new era in business commerce. Working together through their BPMS, the network members can drive value through superior process execution. Speed, quality, flexibility, customization, and cost improve as the business partners find the way to establish communication and share vital information through whatever standards or system is chosen. The transformation will not be limited by industry either. Any firm of any size in any industry can choose to function as a nucleus firm or a node on a network driven by such a channel master. Customized solutions for key customers and targeted consumer groups and the agility to perform will result from componentizing your business processing as well as your software. Businesses and their partners will then function at world-class levels.

Advancement to level 4 and higher now becomes feasible as the linked partners focus not on best practices to help each company individually but on how the network processing can be optimized and the customers satisfied better than any competing network. The hidden capabilities of each partner will surface and be used to enhance the end-to-end capabilities of the combined entity. In this chapter, we have depicted the elements that make BPM such a powerful tool. In the next chapter, we will consider how IT comes directly into the implementation of this new capability.

6

ACHIEVE INFORMATION TECHNOLOGY VALUE THROUGH PROCESS MANAGEMENT

The picture we have been painting is one of firms coming together in a collaborative manner, sharing their insights and critical information, so that together they can build profitable revenues, better utilize joint assets, optimize costs and operating conditions, and satisfy targeted customers and consumer groups better than any competitors. This new and enriched environment, into which firms intent on going beyond supply chain to networked enterprises will move, is part of the higher level sector of an advanced supply chain management (ASCM) effort. The breakthrough enabling the movement, from what can be a stalled position in the evolution, is business process management (BPM) and the systems (BPMS) it introduces for connecting businesses together in a networked fashion. A core technology is a standard language for describing business processes such as Business Process Modeling Language (BPML) or Web Services Business Process Execution Language (BPEL). When these elements are brought together and combined with ASCM, a firm and its allies can move to a position of dominance in a particular industry.

Supply chain excellence in this environment will come from the combined ability to make sense of vast amounts of information passing through the network and to use it to build revenues and profits. In the brave new business world being depicted, firms will compete less on price and more on the use of knowledge to gain:

- **Flexibility**: The ability to adapt processes to meet other partner, key customer, and changing market needs
- **Agility**: The ability to alter processes on demand and meet short-term necessities better than other networks
- **Transparency**: The ability to provide process visibility and control of ongoing processes to selected supply chain partners and key customers
- **Speed**: The ability to do all of the above quickly
- **Quality**: The ability to do the above at high levels of performance, without mistakes and errors in the processing

In previous chapters, we elaborated on the conditions that can occur in the higher levels of ASCM and delved into some of the characteristics behind BPM, which enable the advanced benefits to be achieved. Now we need to move deeper into the details and attributes of the three elements, and especially into how information technology (IT), as a discipline, can use the tools to directly enhance the processing that firms could accomplish, as they connect themselves and share what is necessary to build and execute superior business techniques. As the movement is pursued, we will illustrate many of the features and characteristics of the enriched world being envisioned.

To begin, one of the major results accruing to firms that have successfully applied BPM is that they have eliminated the need to depend on monolithic, stovepipe technology applications. Until recently, IT was restricted in what it could do to help businesses respond to what we have depicted as relentless customer demands, through networked responses and solutions. Existing technologies simply took too long, cost too much, and there were too many political obstacles to overcome. Now, BPM technologies become the methodology that provides the ability to quickly configure the correct interenterprise IT infrastructure needed to support the desired redesigned processes.

BPM has also reduced the lag between management intentions and execution. A major feature has been the speed with which processes can be completed, dramatically enhancing a directly executable business model, while leveraging the firm's existing IT structure, especially its enterprise resource planning system. Now the results are more concrete and responsive to market and customer needs. In this chapter, we will explain the technical details behind these new breakthroughs.

The "Killer App" for BPM Systems Is the Shared Process

For anyone who has been involved in efforts to make agreements between different businesses about the exchange of information, the idea of a shared business process may seem like a joke or a complete nightmare. We tend to think of processes as detailed descriptions of how work is accomplished, like finding all of the hidden work details that had to be discovered and rationalized in the reengineering efforts of the 1980s and early 1990s. If we had to work from the bottom up in an organization, in a similar fashion to find everything we had to accomplish with everyone in our supply chain, then we could give up productive work altogether and just do process workshops for the rest of our business lives. Fortunately, things are not that bad. If we want to make useful supply chain agreements internally and externally, we just have to think of processes in a different manner. We should work from the top down and keep the agreements as simple as possible.

The key issue in this type of effort is determining who does what. That means the first thing to agree on is the overall shape of the improved "process" from end to end, and then who is going to perform which pieces of the process must be determined. After that, the parties agree on the handover points, or what is necessary to complete each activity and what is going to be handed off to start the next part of the processing. Once this "public interface" is accepted, and each party has a working implementation of its own pieces, you have a working shared process. This simple level of agreement is all that is required, although other issues will rapidly arise, with BPM providing a way to handle the most important situations.

Enablement of the implementation comes in many forms, but none so critical as providing visibility to the processing. With BPM, each party can keep control of its own way of working, so long as it conforms to the basic agreement. In principle, the parties could keep their internal processes entirely secret. In practice, much of the advantage of shared process management comes from being able to see into your partner's business. Logistics companies, for example, allow their customers to see where their packages have gotten to and, if the partners are using BPMS, to manage their internal processes, diverting shipments, expediting some over others, and so forth. With visibility into what is happening, the same management can then be done for any thread of business activity.

Yet another issue of importance is validation. It is easy to provide visibility without surrendering control of internal processes, but there may be good reasons for doing exactly that. Many businesses must guarantee that their activities are conducted in a certain way (pharmaceuticals and financial services, for example), and others may well want to build the same kind of assurance into their agreements with partners. BPM offers a way of handling some complex issues of collaborative working, but it also allows the parties to take them apart and handle them one by one. Where proprietary information must be withheld, the parties discuss this issue early, agree on what can or cannot be shared, and then construct the shared processing that helps both parties.

In summary, there are many aspects beneficial to shared processes through BPMS, but none so important as facilitating critical actions within and across enterprises. While BPM technology can be used to manage any business process, its capabilities are most needed when many systems, departments, or businesses must work together to perform a process. Several examples from different industries illustrate the possibilities:

- Private healthcare processes: A physician must check with the payer or provider organization before prescribing a drug or authorizing some other treatment.
- Straight through processing in financial services: A broker places a trade on behalf of an investor, a market marker arranges the sale, and a custodian bank arranges the funds transfer.
- Logistics management: The logistics provider is responsible for finding the least costly route that will meet the contractual commitments of the shipper to the buyer.
- Managed care referral services: An insurance company provides a referral to a service provider that can meet the customer needs and tracks the service while the care is being provided.

In each of these cases, the processes within a firm require the coordinated effort of many individuals, working in different parts of the business and using different information systems. They all share a customer that demands the ability to come to any one of them and know the state of the process: Where is my claim? Where is my order? What was the selling price of my shares? When will I see the product at my site? Where do I send back what I do not want? On a larger scale, when a firm goes beyond supply chain and into the realm of the networked enterprise, the challenge increases. Multiple companies must cooperate and coordinate activities, to answer the same questions and ensure that customers and end consumers get what they want, when they want it. These partners must also allow customers to view progress, make changes, and receive what they need in the shortest possible cycle time. To answer customer questions and meet the needs of a network, we must face another issue. The shared processes require a common language for effective communication. That becomes BPML.

The Enabler for Shared Processes Is a Common Process Language Such as BPML

The Business Process Management Initiative (BPMI.org) was conceived during the spring and summer of 2000. It was initiated by Intalio, Inc. and finally created in August 2000 by a group of 16 software vendors and consulting firms, including Computer Sciences Corporation (CSC). Membership is open to all companies, nonprofit organizations, and individuals. BPMI.org has blossomed as an independent organization and is now made up of over 160 businesses devoted to the development of open specifications for the management of e-business processes that span multiple applications, multiple corporate departments, and multiple business partners, with the ability to conduct business processing either behind a firewall or over the Internet.

One specific intention of the initiative was to develop a solution that would allow businesses to share the definition and management of distributed processes. Accomplishing this intention would not only make business processing more feasible, the developers believed, it would lead to the creation of a language that would greatly facilitate e-commerce collaboration and advanced supply chain efforts. One of the key deliverables from this intention was BPML, a business process modeling language, which became the key to collaboration among companies, applications, and software products.

Before pursuing the details of the language, however, it is important to point out a bit more about intentions. BPMI.org is not designed to be totally independent. Indeed, it complements service initiatives such as J2EE and simple object application protocol (SOAP) that enable legacy infrastructures to converge toward process-oriented enterprise computing and processing initiatives such as ebXML, RosettaNet, BizTalk, Web Services Description Language (WSDL), universal description, discovery, and integration (UDDI), tpaML, and E-Speak that support process-oriented business-to-business collaboration. BPMI.org defines open specifications such as the BPML and the Business Process Query Language (BPQL) that are meant to enable the standards-based management of e-business processes with forthcoming BPMS, in much the same way that SQL enabled the standards-based management of business data using off-the-shelf database management systems.

BPMI.org's offspring, BPML, then becomes a new standard that allows businesses to manage shared processes. But we must keep in mind that it is a language designed for computer systems rather than people. Different disciplines want to and will interact with BPMS using tool sets that "speak their language" in terms that are relevant to their industry. Unfortunately in the past, the absence of an effective standard and the lack of a common language to express complex business processes hindered the development and adoption of e-business. Various standards were available for the correct interpretation of specific pieces of data and specific messages, but there was no way to orchestrate an extended business "conversation" of the kind that really enables business-to-business interaction.

BPML is not the only candidate for a common process language. Another widely accepted standard is BPEL, developed in the summer of 2002 by major software vendors such as IBM, Microsoft, Oracle, and BEA as part of their Web services offering. These vendors developed BPEL to overcome the limitations of existing Web services standards. The initial Web services standards such as SOAP and WSDL were useful for defining what a component could do, but provided no support for orchestrating the work of software components. Initial Web services applications assumed that each business would write code to manage the components. BPEL provides process language to manage how the components work together. As announced, this language is a subset of BPEL, providing less support for complex processes. However, the language is new and the specifications plan enhancements that will likely close the gap over the next two years. The good news for businesses thinking of using either technology is that the underlying mathematics and computer science are the same. More importantly, since both are expressed as XML, firms will have little difficulty in translating a process expressed in one of these process languages into the other standard. BPEL is now under the supervision of the OASIS Web Services Business Process Execution Language Technical Committee.

Developing the integration solution started with an understanding that complex businesses inevitably end up with multiple physical sources of the same data and the complications that occur with process definitions, nonstandard data transfer, and disparate software applications. The original dream of database gurus was that businesses would have a single source for all their business data, but in practice every business unit, and ultimately every application, had a database of its own with no overall control. When different business units, or indeed different businesses, wanted to collaborate closely, they immediately came up against this obstacle of multiple data sources in different languages. The problem was how to align these systems and keep them aligned so that they are effectively integrated into a single virtual source of reliable information.

BPML, or another BPM language, resolves the issue by providing the exchange standard by which process management systems will be able to transfer and align process definitions. The inherent standards are designed from the start, not just to integrate systems and people in their own domain, but also to connect with each other so that process components in different domains can be connected to create a manageable distributed process. At its core, BPML is a machine process language, used to define business components and not intended to be read by humans. BPM requires that teams of people drawn from different disciplines work together to design and implement new processes.

Process designers, for example, tend to work with graphical representations, while business managers think in terms of metrics and process outcomes. Now, these groups can interact through BPMS, using tool sets that speak their language and in terms taken from the industry vocabulary. BPML or other BPM languages contain a mathematical logic that facilitates large-scale interenterprise network collaboration, with the participants operating as peers in the system. Firms such as DuPont, Kraft Foods, Ford, Tesco, and Nestlé, can operate as a nucleus firm or channel master, and their tier 1 or tier 2 suppliers can collaborate with equal abilities. That is one of the real beauties of using BPML in a networked environment: it has advantages for all players.

Raw BPML and other process languages were also not designed to be useful to the designers and managers mentioned. They are intended for

	Material Processes (Things)	Information Processes (Data)	Business Processes (Relationships)
Purpose	Transform and assemble raw materials and components into other components and finished products using resources	Store, retrieve, manipulate, display, and communicate structured and unstructured data and knowledge	Articulate and complete conditions of satisfaction in interactions between customers and performers
Characteristics	Based on the traditions of industrial engineering	Based on the traditions of computer science and software engineering	Based on structures of human communication and coordination found in all languages and cultures
Verbs	Assemble, transform, transport, store, inspect	Send, transact, invoke, save, forward, query	Request, promise, offer, decline, propose, cancel, measure

Figure 6.1 Process Modeling Language Must Support Three Processes (Source: CSC's Research Services)

very precise interpretation by computers and for exchange of definitions between systems. The information needs to be translated into other representations, such as graphics, before people can usefully interpret it. The language also must be very capable. BPML represents business processes and carries the business semantics directly into operational execution. There, it separates process descriptions from software logic so that process management systems can orchestrate the contributions of other systems without having to hard wire them together.

To support the definition and execution of any business process, BPML must be semantically rich enough to represent material flows, information flows, and business commitments. As shown in Figure 6.1, a process modeling language must support and unify three kinds of processes: material, information, and business. It should be able to support the different process paradigms in common use across different industries and unify the various distributed computing models that underpin existing and emerging middleware. It should represent combinations of business-to-business collaboration and enterprise application integration, and it must consolidate workflow processes with automated procedures, to allow the integration of hosted applications, such as Web services.

In addition to accomplishing these tasks, BPML is designed to:

- Expose existing back-end systems and software application logic as business processes
- Allow a process engine to integrate with existing messaging, transaction (middleware), and database management systems
- Support the interchange of processes off-line (packaged processes) as well as on-line (peer to peer)
- Enable processes to react to events and adapt to changing business requirements in real time
- Simplify the management of interactions between processes running on disparate systems and across different business domains
- Enable the rapid development and deployment of new processes, by combining existing process components into new value-added processes
- Enable IT to combine best-of-breed solutions, such as visual process modeling tools, process engines, process management systems, and process analysis tools

BPML in essence becomes the foundation for other process standards. It is a meta-language that offers a generic execution model for business processes that can be translated into more concrete and specific languages that apply to vertical domains. The developers of BPML recognized the importance of leveraging existing standards and technologies within BPML, including standards for the exchange of information and events, business transactions, service advertising and discovery, real-time collaboration, and Web services. In Figure 6.2, we can see how BPML powers the convergence of enterprise and business-to-business technology standards. IT systems are converged with process management and the tools of business-to-business collaboration. This integration occurs, moreover, across two domains: process execution facilities and process development facilities.

BPML will no doubt become the basis of more specialized languages. The result will be a global process network available to any industry. BPMS will become process nodes for the resulting extended enterprises, connecting businesses together in the design and execution of their pro-

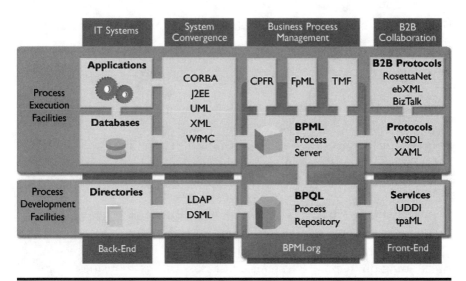

Figure 6.2   BPML Semantics Reflect Process, Industry, and Middleware Diversity (Source: Intalio, Inc.)

cesses. Specific industries will probably form subnetworks with specialized kinds of collaboration, but ultimately everyone will be connected. And the beauty of it is that it won't cost the earth.

Case Studies Illustrate the Power of BPMS

BPM makes it possible to have both the efficiency you need and the process diversity and flexibility that your customers desire. One European conglomerate set up a new business with 160 processes and 127 package applications in 7 months. This European cable company wanted to establish a new company, to provide bandwidth on demand to business customers, but did not want to wait the 17 months quoted by the systems integrators it asked to help jump-start the new business.

The conglomerate's objective was to set up its new business to exploit thousands of kilometers of unused fiber optic cable by offering managed bandwidth solutions to other entities and allowing customers to configure the bandwidth, on demand, over the Web. The market was hot at the time, and customers were ready to buy. But implementing the conglomerate's 14-page business strategy required 160 business processes to be defined and designed, and integration involved numerous

IT systems running 127 third-party best-of-breed applications from commercial off-the-shelf vendors. With this level of complexity, traditional point-to-point systems integration was not feasible. Systems integrators quoted 17 months or more, with little guarantees of success. Using BPM, the new business was launched in seven and one-half months.

The conglomerate brought in the Consulting and Systems Integration group of CSC's U.K. division to help with the effort. Using Catalyst, a top-down process design methodology, CSC and the new business developed a coherent process model for the business. They also developed a unique BPM architecture (see Figure 6.3) to support this new way of deploying IT systems. The model was then used to guide the systems integrations. The commercial off-the-shelf packages were linked through quickly written "adapters" attached to "spokes" on a "hub" directed by the business process. Significant functionality, such as data mapping, was extracted and performed by a shared service. This top-down integration sped up development and made it easier to change packages when required.

A new framework used products from BEA (Tuxedo, Web Logic, and Elink) and a workflow management product from Staffware. The team selected commercial applications from 12 vendors, abstracted the business processes from these components, and migrated them into a business process engine that was built into the framework. With this structure, business processes are configured in one central function rather than hard coded in many applications. Since the processes drive the execution of the applications, it was possible to create a consistent user interface, including a single sign-on through a common Web portal that supports many different devices. Four hundred application screens were "re-faced" to conform. Smart product choices along with a good process methodology and attention to architecture have wide applications.

This framework, which is now called CSC's e4, in which explicit business processes drive systems, is widely applicable to other industries and provides significant benefits in terms of speed, control, and flexibility. Components are easily switched in or out, reducing dependency on specific vendors and providing a smoother path to legacy migration.

BPM Architecture Offers Many Possibilities

Intalio is just one of three companies that have announced standards-based BPMS, but this firm has been at the forefront of developing the

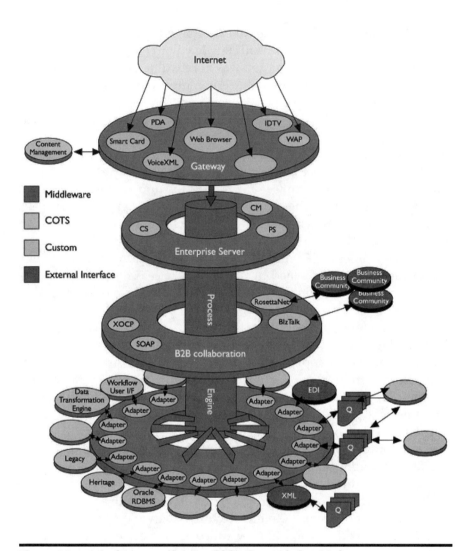

Figure 6.3   e4 Architecture (Source: CSC's Research Services)

enabling architecture (see Figure 6.4). The firm uses BPML to directly execute business models that include people, systems, and other organizations. Its architectural version, dubbed n3, is scalable, in both directions, upward to include multiple large-scale servers distributed across multiple organizations and downward to support small pilots and experiments. For small-scale efforts, n3 allows the use of open source software to substitute for the commercial components that are typically

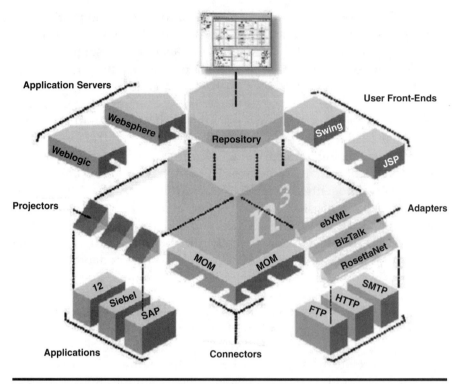

Figure 6.4   Directly Executing Business Models (Source: Intalio, Inc.)

used. Going forward, CSC's e4 team is looking to make extensive use of BPML and is currently reviewing Intalio's n3, which can directly execute BPML.

BPML implementations bring process management to existing and future IT investments. A declarative semantics and a distributed concurrent processing model were chosen by the designers, so the process management systems that supported BPML could provide end-to-end process analysis, prediction, simulation, and metrics, spanning multiple business applications and business partners and providing visibility across all participants.

BPM Leverages Your Investment In Componentized Architecture

Every business has a legacy or heritage IT. This term was once used for older homegrown investments to distinguish them from the new generation of applications that would soon bring productivity and profitability to a business. In reality, many businesses have a large base of installed IT that has not fulfilled promises or met expectations but somehow does not seem to be able to adapt to the fast-paced changing demands of today's market. The good news is that the technology vendors have changed the way they license software. These changes are designed to allow you to support business processes that require support from people, multiple applications, and other businesses.

If you are using enterprise applications such as SAP, Oracle, PeopleSoft, Siebel, or any middleware product, the vendors are already moving to components and to service-based architectures. Where once they would have resisted any attempt to access their software at the component level, they now merely ask you how you would like to access their software. The choices are usually a mixture of a proprietary data format, traditional enterprise application (connector or adaptor architecture), and/or some type of XML messaging. They now also support Web services access.

Web services is the name for a common framework for defining software components and invoking them using standards based on public Internet protocols. They can be used singly or strung together to provide more complex business services. Because the many standards (XML, SOAP, UDDI, and others) are open and the communication infrastructure is public and pervasive, components defined in this way can communicate with one another even if they run on different platforms, were developed in different languages, and even reside in different organizations. Web services are now available both to create new components and to expose bits of packages and legacy applications in this new way.

The Web services standard provides a useful tool for creating, publishing, and accessing many common business services, such as:

- A request for a share price or a quotation, which is a one-shot transaction for which Internet access is useful and there is no need to track an extended process.
- A call for product details where the information is dynamic but the call itself is static. Such calls could be integrated with a customer or employee portal.
- Publishing updates to customer information so that various applications (call center system, customer order management, and so forth) can be simultaneously updated. Simple messaging can support very limited forms of systems integration.

BPMS work perfectly well with Web services components, integrating them into larger processes, but they have a number of practical limitations, which should be kept in mind. Some of these limitations are overcome by using Web service components with BPM:

- Performance remains an issue for services delivered using Internet protocols, especially over public interfaces. For the time being, Web services are not suited for high transaction volumes.
- There is no built-in security in the Web services architecture, and it remains an unsolved issue. You can add security to the application, but in doing so you add cost and complexity and you lose the advantage of universal applicability.
- Initially, Web services provided very limited information about the internal activities of components and how they were executed. A programmer invoking a Web service needed to know how the underlying applications worked or risked getting unanticipated results.

In the spring of 2002, an additional standard, the Web Services Choreography Interface (WSCI), was released to bridge the gap between BPM and Web services, by describing how a Web service can be used as part of a larger, more complex business process. However, Web services components do not hold information about the state of each instance of the process, and they are therefore not suited for use in applications where you need visibility of what is going on inside the components. This was followed in the summer of 2002 by the announcement of BPEL.

BPM does not provide a common trading language, but there are other new technologies that will help break through this final barrier. With BPM and components architecture, you and your trading partners can design and deploy processes at the click of a mouse. You can share information, but the question becomes how you know that you really understand each other. Do you both use the word "customer" in the same way? What about "payment" or "delivery" or any of the many complex terms that make up a business contract? Come to think of it, did that order for an "apple" mean fruit or a computer? Computer scientists call this the ontology problem: How do we know that words have the same meaning across and within businesses? For the rest of us, this is the complex "data" issue that always seems to get in the way of working together. The good news is that a new generation of data modeling and integration tools has made it easier to tackle this problem.

Early efforts to conduct business electronically among partners, suppliers, and customers were accelerated by the use of a standard, called XML, for the way that items were described. On April 25, 1998, the *Economist* wrote:

> ...But the biggest role that XML is expected to play is in integrating the way that existing paper documents — invoices, loan applications, contracts, insurance claims, you name it — are exchanged between organizations around the world. Imagine what the world would be like if one company's computer system could automatically read any other organization's documents — and make complete sense of them? This is the goal that the technique known as EDI has struggled, unsuccessfully, to achieve for years. Though efforts have barely begun, there is a chance that XML could actually make that happen. If it did, business on the Web could run riot.

However, as discussed in CSC's Research Services' *Foundation Research Journal* in November 2000, there are some concerns about how widely shared the meaning of terms used in e-business is. This is known as the ontology problem.

Nowhere in this easily machine-readable format is there any clue as to what is meant by any of the tags. For example, <Disk> could be a floppy, a hard disk, a removable device, or something else entirely. There is no explicit statement of the context. As noted XML expert Robin Cover says, "...descriptive markup (such as XML) proves to be of limited relevance as a mechanism to enable information interchange at the level of the machine" (XML and SemanticTransparency, http:// xml.coverpages.org/xmlndSemantics.html). The problem becomes significantly worse, indeed potentially fatal, when dealing with other cultures and languages. For example, see the advertisements at www.engrish.com, especially the toiletries section where the words are correct, but the context is unexpected.

In the corporate world, this problem is expressed in the length of time it takes to convert data from one system to another. For example, when American Airlines took over TWA, many traveling businesspeople were concerned about what would happen to their frequent flyer miles. TWA was one of the few U.S. airlines that flew to a number of cities. Travelers based in one of these cities were understandably concerned.

American Airlines responded by saying that all frequent flyer miles would be carried over to the American frequent flyer program. However, this took an entire year to accomplish. With a product called Coherence from Unicorn Solutions (www.unicorn.com), this transformation could have been much more rapid.

Coherence provides an environment that lets a skilled knowledge engineer build a model of the data for an idealized airline frequent flyer program. Once this model is created, then the specifics of a particular database, XML schema, or application program interface are mapped to the idealized model. Think of it as going from a "many-to-many" solution, where each database had to be mapped to each other database, to a "hub-and-spoke" solution, where each node on a spoke is mapped just once to the hub. Once mapped, Coherence is able to automatically generate the transformation between any two nodes in either SQL or XSLT. These transformations make it possible to go immediately from one data source to another, either in batch production mode or on the fly to support ad-hoc analysis.

ChipCo-Global Found That Developing a Common Language Grew Profits and Customer Satisfaction

ChipCo-Global proved that ontology is more than interesting abstraction. Attacking data integrity problems resulted in dramatic improvements in customer satisfaction and profits. The company believed its costly planning and production problems were in large part due to one common issue — a "jungle" of inconsistent planning and production databases.

ChipCo-Global is a global business, in terms of customers, suppliers, and production. Close coordination is required to deliver products, on time and on budget, everywhere in the world. Problems in coordination create unhappy customers, which drives down profits. Classical solutions, such as increased stock-to-buffer problems in production, also drive down profits.

Adding to this coordination difficulty is the fact that ChipCo-Global's business is complex, made up of many apparently similar products that in fact turn out to have different uses. For example, with high-density chips, you don't know what speed you will get from a production lot. Only after you have tested do you know what you have and what part of your orders you can fill. The result is a "jungle" of databases.

ChipCo-Global is committed to giving each customer exactly what it wants. This puts pressure on ChipCo-Global's ability to plan across many systems and many databases. For example, the production schedule quantity for a certain customer for a certain work week exists in five different systems. If these systems experience data integrity issues, it can cause many different kinds of trouble.

ChipCo-Global found a new tool for data modeling that increased the speed and accuracy of its ability to spot and resolve data integrity issues when the Planning Group in one of the fabrication facilities decided that it was time to take some action. The initial idea was to start making an explicit comparison of data items to identify data integrity issues and to assess the status of the data integrity.

To foster this effort, the group developed an initiative called the Integrity Quality Monitor (IQM), which implemented an engine to compare information from two different systems. The IQM engine examines the way that the data are handled, with different naming conventions and different values for the category construction. In the first stage, IQM was limited to two systems for comparison. The SQL scripts to feed the engine were developed manually.

Experience with the first-stage comparisons led ChipCo-Global to understand that there was a broad generic need for systems data integrity monitoring. To address this need, ChipCo-Global developed a second-stage generic IQM comparison engine built on a generic structure for data comparison management and Web reporting.

The increased comparison capability of the second-stage IQM required a more powerful means of generating the SQL scripts for input. Unicorn's Coherence proved to be a very time- and cost-effective way to bring all the different business logic calculations and naming conventions together in a way that worked with the common baseline used by the comparison engine.

Coherence functions by constructing a high-level model of the information and then mapping specific instances to the high-level model. Once these modeling and mapping tasks are completed, Coherence can automatically generate the appropriate transformations between any two sets of information. This transformation can be expressed as SQL, XML, or in direct API-to-API conversion.

ChipCo-Global wanted to test if Unicorn's Coherence would be able to model such a complex set of relations. Initially ChipCo-Global was very sceptical and expected that it would take a long time to capture the business logic, which was not at all obvious from the outside. However,

Central Information Model

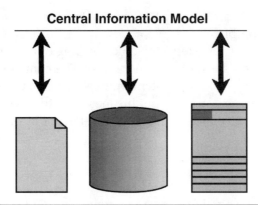

Figure 6.5 Single Strategy View: Through Unicorn's Coherence, Data Formats Can Be Linked to Other Data Formats, By Leveraging a Central Ontology Model

in practice, it only took a couple of meetings with the information modeler from Unicorn to explain the business logic. Once that was completed, ChipCo-Global provided Unicorn with the database schemas and examples of the data. Much to ChipCo-Global's surprise, two days later, the Unicorn staff was back with the model and able to generate the SQL between any pair of databases. This provided ChipCo-Global with the input it needed to feed databases into its generic IQM evaluation engine.

A review of what Unicorn did during those two days to develop the high-level model of the data convinced ChipCo-Global that once it became familiar with the way that Coherence works, it too would be able to develop its own models in a brief period of time. In making use of Coherence, ChipCo-Global realized that it was not minimizing the need for intellectual work but rather making use of a tool that let the company extract maximum value from work it had already done.

ChipCo-Global struck pay dirt when it conducted its comparison of the Plan of Record (POR) system and a new shipping system. The POR system is a legacy system that handles the fabrication schedules for what is made at which locations and on which days. The new shipping system is responsible for internal shipment within ChipCo-Global. It allows sharing from one part of the supply chain to the next. It carries the information about what day, what quantity, and where to ship.

By using Coherence to create inputs to its IQM comparison engine, ChipCo-Global discovered a major bug in how the end-of-the-month process was handled. The company discovered that it used the wrong schedule, which then routinely triggered extensive manual intervention to clear up the problem.

ChipCo-Global's next step is to look at rolling out this new capability to other fabrication sites around the world. The company is optimistic that although the planning system "jungle" of databases will always exist, due to the complexity of its business, for the first time ChipCo-Global will be able to model, analyze, and ferret out problems.

Conclusions

The breakthrough enabling firms to move to level 3 of supply chain and beyond is BPM and the systems it introduces for connecting businesses in a networked manner. Firms then compete less on price and more on the use of knowledge, as they move from stovepipe technology applications to quickly configuring the correct interenterprise infrastructure needed to support the processing desired by the intended customers. From the business perspective, BPM reduces the lag between management intention and successful execution, facilitating critical actions within and across the linked enterprises. The critical element becomes the BPML applied by the collaborating firms.

7

BPM RESULTS COME IN A VARIETY OF FLAVORS: MOVING TO LEVELS 4 AND 5

In this chapter, we want to delve into two scenarios. First, a business process management system (BPMS) can be driven by a nucleus firm (like Wal-Mart, Kraft Foods, or General Motors), accepting that it will take time for standards to be accepted by the partners and there will be the inevitable slowness of some supply chain partners to get prepared for collaboration. Under these conditions, the nucleus firm can move forward with business process management (BPM), for its own progress, with the help of a select group of trusted allies. Advantage will come to the firm by carefully extending the effort, to get more end-to-end visibility in the supply chain and to gain control through better feedback on what is happening across the network. From this perspective, the benefits for the nucleus firm, acting alone, will be considerable and the assisting partners generally increase their positions with the grateful nucleus firm, although there is little in the way of long-term guarantees.

The second choice is for a nucleus firm to instigate a full network movement and to use BPM to link many partners in an end-to-end fashion as they enable themselves and their allies to collaborate. Using its scale to drive the effort, the nucleus firm works with its key suppliers, design partners, distributors, and enablers to gain a market advantage with specific business customers, such as a large retailer. In the most advanced types of this secondary choice, the effort is extended with the help of a key customer, to design an extended enterprise network focused on specific consumer groups. In the latter case, all parties are expected to use technology and collaboration to create a network clearly different from the competition in the eyes of the end consumers. This condition is the most difficult to establish.

For example, in the first instance, a DuPont could put in one system for buyers to use with many customers, perhaps through an industry exchange such as Elemica. Target Stores could keep its information close to itself and share what is necessary with a limited number of suppliers through a private portal. In either of these cases, the nucleus firm encourages suppliers to use Business Process Modeling Language (BPML), to reduce the cost of participation and to facilitate entry and collaboration in a networked environment.

In the second instance, a Kraft Foods could work with its key suppliers of labels, packaging, and ingredients, a few distributors, and logistics enablers to design a network system focused on Kroger or Wal-Mart. In the advanced effort, Kraft could work directly with Wal-Mart, to develop an integrated supply chain effort. This work could include jointly planned promotions, efforts to achieve pricing optimization, consumer direct marketing, and focused new product development. These types of efforts require on-line visibility, real-time access to trend data, and extremely short and reliable cycle times for all of the critical process steps.

As we progress through this chapter, many examples will be used to illustrate how the desire to move forward with one or the other of these scenarios is being accomplished, as a few pathfinders step out and begin using BPM as the systems enabler. The difference between what these leaders are accomplishing and the competitors are failing to achieve can be measured in years, not months. The leaders, moreover, are locking up positions with key supply chain constituents that will be very difficult for the laggards to overcome. The process begins by taking a hard look at existing systems and business models and instigating a design of something contemporary.

Core Processes Will Be Best for Each Customer, or the Firm Will Outsource

In a first move toward the two conditions being considered, BPM technologies will be used to blow up old business models, particularly as they relate to achieving dominance through core processes. The trend will be more toward doing what a firm is absolutely first or second best at and looking for help with everything else. BPM technology provides a fast and cost-effective platform for integrating business capabilities — specific skills and knowledge — into an organized set of business activities, which makes the federated, networked, enterprise business model feasible in any industry. Using BPM, a nucleus firm can integrate a set of capabilities into a customized business process that delivers the precise set of goods and services the targeted customer wants, at a better price and speed than the old less than fully integrated business can deliver.

Virtual, flexible business networks have been gradually replacing tightly integrated traditional businesses over the last 20 years, as each new wave of technology has reduced the cost of transactions, communications, data retrieval, and storage. The business of the future will be operating around a small core of nucleus firms, which set strategy and control business processes made up of some capabilities the firm performs itself, some performed by others, and some performed with others. For example, DuPont once saw itself as a large vertical business with core competencies in each business unit, supported on occasion with a few joint ventures. Today, the chemical giant has a much smaller set of core competencies, supported by an ever-changing set of businesses that are acquired, spun off, developed through joint ventures, or established through shared technologies. More importantly, DuPont recognizes that the business capability, not the business unit, is a more useful starting point for working with other businesses within and outside this nucleus firm. The result will be a vastly larger and very different market for business process outsourcing than exists today.

The difference is illustrated in the two conditions described in Figure 7.1. In our example, DuPont is moving from an integrated business model, where it operated and controlled virtually all processing, to a more dynamic business model, where businesses and business components are acquired, divested, created, and brought to market as part of what becomes network services. The result will be new levels of speed, flexibility, and response to customer and consumer needs, with the nucleus firm benefiting from the differentiation it creates in the eyes of the designated customers.

The first difference will be in the range and domain of in-house and outsourced capabilities and processes. The traditional view of outsourcing is summarized in Geoffrey Moore's advice: "Focus on core and outsource

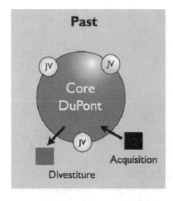 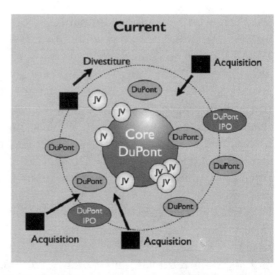

Figure 7.1   Businesses Will Alter Traditional Arrangements (Source: John Taylor)

everything else" (Moore, 2000). Under these conditions, businesses leave the basic support or "context" activities such as payroll, employee benefits, security, and plant maintenance to low-cost providers and focus on the core processes of their business. As "core" has come to mean "what makes your stock price rise," more capabilities and business processes become candidates for outsourcing: customer care (call centers, returns, new product launch), warehousing, logistics, and other aspects of supply chain management. In addition, some companies work with other businesses on specific projects such as contract research, product development, a sales campaign, or a special promotional event. Deciding whether to outsource a capability or a process will not depend on whether it is core or context, but whether your business can do the process well or needs to work with another which does the process better.

The second difference will be that businesses will sell outsourced services as well as buy them. A business that has a world-class capability can leverage its return on investment by taking that capability to market, possibly even to competitors. The old distinctions between buyers/sellers and competitors/partners break down under these conditions, creating new opportunities and new risks, particularly in industries that do not have a history of cooperation.

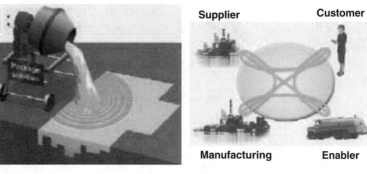

Yesterday	From Now On
Standard Processes	Mass Customized Processes
Clear Boundaries	Rich Collaboration
Servicce Levels	Balanced Scorecard
Fee for Service	Shared Risk and Reward
By Request	Proactive Marketing
Standard Applications	Business Process Management
and Infrastucture	Infrastucture

Figure 7.2   Business Process Outsourcing Changes a Business from a Service to an Active Partnership (Source: CSC's Research Services)

The third difference will be the transition from standard commodity processes to highly customized, agile processes, as described in Figure 7.2. Business process outsourcers will compete on their ability to customize processes to the needs of their customer's customer in specific markets. Both the nucleus firm and the outsourcer will expect these needs to change, and the outsourcing agreement will specify how the customer's requirements will be monitored and how decisions will be made to modify business processes accordingly. The transition goes from standard processes delivered on request with clear boundaries for each process step to mass-customized processes, with rich collaboration and a balanced scorecard to make certain the risk and rewards are equitably shared.

Finally, the relationship between the buyer and seller, backed up by shared metrics and risk and reward contracts, will become much richer. Once business process outsourcing moves from support activities into processes that directly affect the customer or consumer, all parties in the relationship, especially the end consumer, will demand visibility into the process, at least at the level of the transaction affecting them. These conditions will change how business process outsourcing is bought and sold. Today, outsourcing is usually in response to a buyer's Request For Proposal. The goal is to provide a standard best practice, primarily to reduce cost and possibly to improve service. In the future, business process outsourcing will be focused on a flexible response to specific customer requirements.

There are already many examples of nucleus firms offering core competencies as an outsourced process. Procter & Gamble will put its world-class marketing organization to work on your existing new product launch. P&G will use its Vulcan diagnostics to provide you with a blueprint for increasing the efficiencies of your manufacturing organization. DuPont will provide you with a safety program for your manufacturing organization. International Flavors and Fragrances will use its global research on taste preferences of today's children to help you decide the snack food for the next generation.

Expect More Collaboration Between Businesses — And Fewer Mergers and Acquisitions

As the movement toward nucleus firms taking the central role in process management continues, there will be another trend of importance, one in which mergers become less important than collaboration for network benefit. Businesses spent $8.7 trillion on mergers and acquisitions in the 1990s, and well over half of these deals failed to enhance stockholder value or live up to their promises. Many actually reduced stockholder value. Many companies are now attempting to divest recent acquisitions, while others are finding that neither investors nor industry analysts are confident that mergers will solve their problems.

Our research* shows that information technology (IT) strategy is an important factor in the success or failure of mergers and acquisitions, and we have strongly advised companies to adopt one of four IT strategies — consolidation, combination, transformation, or preservation — early in the deal making, to assess the risks and costs of the proposed deal more accurately. Before BPM, all of these strategies were difficult, expensive, and risky. Our report cited successful examples of each strategy, but all were exceptional. In Figure 7.3, the typical conditions en-

---

* Managing IT Through Mergers and Acquisitions, Foundation Report 114, August 1997.

IT Strategy	Before BPM	Now
Consolidation Processes and systems of one company are applied to another.	This invariably took more time and cost more than was budgeted, especially where the two companies had different versions of the same ERP system.	You can consolidate processes while using BPM to leverage the existing systems.
Combination Best-of-breed processes and systems are identified and deployed.	This was an elegant concept, but tedious and time consuming because middleware layers had to be crafted to integrate processes across application boundaries; people-based processes were ignored or supported to separate workflow systems.	BMP provides a platform for integrating both people and systems; projects will cost less and take less time. A top-down, process-driven approach increases the likelihood that process goals are well understood and achieved.
Transformation The entire organization is reinvented, with new processes and new applications.	This minimized the need to integrate the new with the old, but replacing everything is risky.	BMP reduces the risk of this approach because a company can focus on one process area at a time; however, imposing new processes on old systems is risky and expensive.
Preservation Existing processes and systems are preserved in acquired and acquiring companies.	This required strong communication and management metrics to support joint goal setting and performance monitoring. This approach spawned data warehousing projects that could not collect or transform data quickly enough for real-time decision making.	BPM provides greater visibility and control at the transaction and management levels. Unlike today's middleware or workflow technologies, BPM provides a path for businesses to work together and share information even when they do not have the same processes and systems. Collection and sharing of metrics are easier since processes are tracked end to end.

Figure 7.3   From an IT Perspective, BPM Reduces the Risk and Cost (Source: CSC's Research Services)

countered in each of the four strategic areas are depicted, with the differences before and after BPM.

BPM will reduce the risk in mergers and acquisitions. First, process change is separated from drastic change in the IT systems of the businesses. Therefore, an organization can focus its resources on changing key processes, not on replacing IT systems. Similarly, businesses that want to transform themselves can focus resources on one process area at a time. Second, BPM provides speed, visibility, and control. Business and IT work together to develop new processes and refine them, while the technology allows them to learn from their people and their customers. BPM also makes it easier to accommodate local processes and factors relating to culture and organizational structure, often the reasons for an acquisition being a success or failure.

BPM assists mergers and acquisitions by making it easy to mix and match capabilities, but it can do the same for business partners, without the risk and cost of a merger. Many merger and acquisition deals put two companies with flaws together, with the expectation that the new company will be better and succeed. In fact, the good parts of the business suffer while management invests time and resources in the poor parts, or the poor parts drag down the performance of the whole enterprise while customers, employees, and shareholders suffer. There is a better scenario, one in which firms identify and then ruthlessly evaluate the components of their business. World-class components are kept and become sources of new revenue in the form of capabilities that will be provided to customers, complementary businesses, even to competitors. Components that are not world class will be sold or shut down.

Partnerships will begin to replace mergers and acquisitions, since the same BPM software that lowers the cost and risk of mergers and acquisitions also reduces the cost and risk of working with partners. These partnerships require little up-front investment and can be more easily terminated if a partner is unwilling or unable to fulfill its obligations. For example, Coca-Cola and Procter & Gamble backed away from a proposed merger of their snack food businesses, which gathered little enthusiasm from either company's stockholders. The two companies have agreed, instead, to use each other's core capabilities. Coca-Cola will distribute Procter & Gamble's snack products and Procter & Gamble will assist Coca-Cola in new product launches. Each company is providing the other with a world-class capability that was once reserved solely for the exclusive use of the nucleus firm.

	Contacted Choice	Coordinated Co-Working	Creative Collaboration
	Provided a product or service	*Providing a capability that operates independently*	*Working together toward a joint goal with joint risk and reward*
Example	Silicon wafer production	Logistics	Designing a new flavor
Role of Suppliers	■ Supplier provides the capability	■ Pick, pack, and ship; some assembly ■ Freight forwarding under rules of many countries ■ Reports package status to customer and customer's customer	■ Participating firms share tools and space ■ BPM may be used to coordinate work and document that work has occurred
Role of BPM	■ Supply chain management ■ Engineering change control	■ Supply chain management ■ Routing and tracking ■ Customs and other management ■ Billing and collections ■ Customer service	■ Scheduling, coordination, and tracking ■ Project documentation design and management ■ Regulatory compliance management

Figure 7.4   Moving Forward with Collaboration (Source: CSC's Research Services)

BPM Makes All Forms of Partnering Easier

Business managers have discovered what those in the IT world have known for some time: an organization built from well-defined components is more versatile and valuable than a single integrated entity or one assembled from elements with poorly defined boundaries and capabilities. Figure 7.4 uses three basic examples to illustrate how a business can move from doing everything itself or selectively outsourcing processes directly to innovative collaboration. This creates an opportunity for a nucleus firm to better utilize the capabilities of external partners or for partners to attach themselves as a node to a nucleus firm and perform an essential activity in the overall supply chain processing.

The secret, of course, is what has been advocated: the componentizing of steps within the processes, so the partners can collaborate in the appropriate manner. There are four basic patterns of business componentization,* similar to those found in software development and providing similar benefits:

- **Unbundling**: Splitting up similar things, such as products and services, so that the parts are worth more than the whole. Business units may be unbundled in preparation for spin-off or sale and products or services segmented to maximize revenue and profits within specific customer segments.
- **Decoupling**: Breaking up groups of different things so that each can be leveraged more effectively. For example, selling products or services through several common channels (the Web, the telephone, and field sales) instead of just one.
- **Paring and genericizing**: Paring an organization down to what it does best and genericizing that function for widespread use within the business or by other businesses. Many businesses now provide a capability that was once internal to other businesses. Services and processes rather than products are the principal source of revenue and profits.
- **Isolating and extracting**: Establishing clean boundaries around areas of the business to make it easier to outsource them (or to insource work from other organizations). Boundary setting is about stabilizing boundaries and setting standards for communication. This has been used extensively in heavy manufacturing and in aerospace, where one or more original equipment manufacturers coordinate the work of hundreds of subcontractors.

BPM Will Allow Business Relationships to Become More Creative

As nucleus firms start to pursue the second avenue to success — establishing network strength benefiting all partners — they will quickly find another trend of benefit: introducing innovative features that further distinguish what the network offers to customers. These features can come from nodal companies helping the nucleus firm reduce cycle times from concept to commercial success, but they come with a caveat: Cre-

---

* See Componentizing Your Software and Your Business, Foundation Strategic Innovation Report, 1998.

ativity cannot be automated. It cannot even be defined and implemented in a process definition. What BPM can do is be used to remove some of the obstacles to creative collaboration. Thus, it makes creativity more feasible if business managers are prepared to take advantage of this tool. The technology makes it possible to work with customers, suppliers, and other partners in richer, more productive and more efficient ways. Systems can be integrated and new processes can be implemented quickly and easily, but establishing the relationships and the management structures to take advantage of this new capability is a subtle and difficult problem.

Collaborations between different organizations take two basic forms:

- **Service provision**: Some of the activities of the different parties can be managed independently; that is, the firms can provide well-defined services to each other. This way of working is perfectly appropriate if the parties have some particular resource or expertise and other parties need no deep knowledge of it in order to buy and use the service. Utilities such as electric, telecommunications, and wide-area networks are obvious examples, and this form clearly includes all services that can be fully automated. The key management issue in this area is "reality." Is the service properly defined? Does the supplier have the right capability? Is this supplier really providing what was specified? Is the price right?

  Relationships like this are handled by specifications, contracts, and service-level agreements. This is easy for commodity services, but there are problems in one-off services, or single-process relationships that require expertise at each point in the handoff, where the expertise of the supplier is needed not just in providing a solution but in defining the problem. When the plumber shakes his head and sucks his teeth, you know you're in trouble.

- **Creative collaboration**: Other activities can only (or at least should only) be carried out together. These will be people-centric activities that include creative problem solving and design where both parties have expertise to contribute and other activities that are mutually dependent. One of the lessons of reengineering was that work can be much more effective if departmental stovepipes are broken down and people get together in multidisciplinary teams to come up with the best possible solution. The same condition applies to creative and collaborative work between businesses. The key management issue in this area is "sponsorship." Are the senior managers committed to the collaboration? Are they putting their best people on the task and encouraging them to engage creatively? Are these managers getting together with their peers, to decide how the result can be exploited most effectively and how the costs and benefits will be shared?

Opportunities for creative collaboration are often missed. Many business relationships sit in unhappy limbo between these two poles. Different departments and different businesses are often assumed to be providing well-defined services to each other, and their interactions are managed by specifications and contracts when their activities are actually deeply interdependent. IT is a particularly important example of this, and it turns into an issue of collaboration between businesses when it is outsourced. The usual giveaways are that the "service" can't quite be defined properly or that work keeps looping backward and forward between the parties because each is tackling one aspect of what is in fact a single problem. BPM helps to expose the creative possibilities in a number of different ways:

- **BPM integrates information sources**: Businesses and departments within them are often seen as "owners" of the information they hold. This is perfectly healthy if it means that they are responsible for its quality, but it can result in a very territorial attitude. It is combinations of information that lead to creative insights. The fragmentation of information in different business areas makes them impossible.

  BPM makes it easy to draw together information from different sources, not just in the technical sense of joining data in different databases but pulling in different kinds of information because they are going to be used together. Integrating product information, market information, and customer information, for example, allows people to ask important and interesting questions and it implies that all these areas of the business should be collaborating to answer them.

- **BPM removes the clutter of routine work**: "Knowledge work," or the use of expertise to solve problems, is often embedded in a welter of more routine processing and administration. This means that experts spend only a small proportion of their time using and honing their real skills. They spend a lot of time in routine drudgery, including the use of multiple, incompatible IT systems, rapidly becoming frustrated and demoralized.

BPM can be used to integrate the systems required and to present the experts with the functionality that they require to do their real work. It can also automate all the routine tasks so that they are left to focus on the areas where their expertise is important. This undoubtedly makes the experts more productive and it makes their jobs more interesting. What it also does is to focus the attention of smart people on the area where they create most value — and where collaboration with other experts may be most valuable.

- **BPM focuses creative attention on processes themselves**: BPM uses a process model to drive business activity. Where processes are shared, this means that the various parties have to collaborate to define what must be accomplished, and the modeling exercise enables them to apply creative energy to improving the work. The process itself becomes the focus for creative collaboration, and once established, this relationship opens up the possibility of other creative activities, such as the development of new product concepts.

- **BPM integrates IT people into the team**: BPM technologies turn processes into a directly implementable IT concept. The process that businesspeople talk about as a way of understanding and taking control of the way the business works is now represented in the IT domain, where it is used directly to resolve the issues in integrating systems. In other words, processes become the focus of attention for both business and IT people, and a common language unites the two domains. The linguistic and conceptual dislocation between IT and the rest of the business, which is often cited as a major obstacle to the creation of value from technology, is overcome. BPM tools create a common domain in which IT and businesspeople can collaborate. As a result, it could revolutionize the value of technology to the business.

Process Operations Will Be Integrated with Process Monitoring

With the acceptance and use of BPM to enhance networked enterprises, firms find another feature. BPM will give a business unprecedented ability to view and control its business process operations and those conducted by the business partners selected for collaboration. This means that either as a nucleus firm driving the network relationships or as a key node to the nucleus firm's activities, there will be better opportunities to take the correct actions at the time of need. Visibility will make process operation information available in real time, to be validated immediately and accessed by anyone with a right to see it: customers, business partners, regulatory agencies, consumer groups. Increasingly, the ability to demonstrate real-time compliance with industry, national, and contractual standards on quality, environmental protection, and safety is required not only to get contracts but also to keep them. BPM delivers this capability, but the firm will be managing in a goldfish bowl.

Any business operates within a complex web of global, national, and local regulations and business contracts that dictate not just what you produce but how you produce it. Each set of regulations requires you to document your processes and demonstrate compliance or face penalties. Today, compliance often requires capturing and storing data from multiple manual and automated systems. Food, for example, is tracked from seed to field to warehouse to processing plant or restaurant. If the process control systems fail or your records are incomplete, your plants may be shut down or your products or services must be withdrawn from the market.

BPM helps you comply with regulations and contractual obligations in three ways. First, BPM eliminates the recording of incomplete or out-of-range data. For example, in clinical drug trials, medical staff writes much of the patient data by hand. If the data are illegible or out of bounds, the entire patient record is disqualified from the trial. BPM technologies can integrate systems that capture data directly from the medical instruments with information collected by humans and provide instant feedback so that out-of-range data can be corrected straight away. Automating routine data validation also releases time and resources for issues that are difficult to measure and need human intervention.

Second, BPM can reduce the cost of compliance for you and for the regulators. Of course, there is the initial investment in BPM, and your own compliance monitors and those from regulatory agencies must guide the design of these systems. But when compliance information is available in a process database, there is less need for monitors to visit local sites to verify that process standards are being meet, so fewer are needed. More importantly, automation of routine compliance will free your compliance monitors to focus on difficulties that are not addressed by automation.

Finally, because BPM stores process transactions in a single integrated database, process monitoring systems can alert your monitors to problems and issues that they would not see if the information were kept in separate databases or paper files and only brought together at intervals. Analysis will pick up patterns in noncompliance that can help diagnose the underlying cause. For example, a meat processor notified that a restaurant serving meat from one of its plants has reported some cases of *E. coli* bacteria infection knows that the source of the outbreak could be the restaurant, the warehouse, the plant, or unrelated to the meat supply. A BPM-based early warning system will help all parties to identify the problem and find a quick remedy.

However, this new level of control raises performance expectations and penalties for failure. Compliance monitoring will no longer be an annual event but rather an everyday real-time process. New regulations will require you to report and remedy problems in real time. If you cannot comply, your plants could be shut down. In areas such as loan processing or insurance claim settlement, violation of due process or legal requirements could quickly accrue hundreds of thousands of dollars in liability for violations of criminal or civil law. BPM gives you more effective tools for designing and controlling your processes, but the consequences for poor execution will be more severe.

Consumers will also have more access to information about your processes. This provides an opportunity to build consumer loyalty through your approach to sensitive issues such as sustainable manufacturing, environmental protection, animal rights, genetic engineering, organic farming, and labor practices. However, the risk of losing business is equally strong. If consumer groups have the right to monitor your compliance records, the value of your business could be destroyed by an isolated incident at one of your sites or that of a business partner.

BPM Provides the Foundation of Analytic Systems

With BPM, management across a network, from a nucleus firm to its suppliers and customers, can see into every aspect of your business processes, including those performed by your firm and with others. For most businesses, this is a major change in both the quality and quantity of information available. BPM transaction information provides rich data to address real-time operational decisions as well as longer term strategy decisions. However, to leverage this information, you need to create an analytic database by extracting and transforming the transaction data into a format that supports decision making. Do not assume your business managers understand that a database optimized for transactions may not easily support analytics: remember how enterprise resource planning systems sold at board level only to be more expensive than anticipated and much more difficult to implement. Often, IT needed millions of extra dollars and a year or more of effort to create the anticipated executive support systems. Make sure that your BPM project plans and budgets include both transaction and analytics capabilities.

You also need the people and tools to make use of this enhanced information sharing. Many everyday analytic tasks are complex and will require you to build or buy complicated applications. These analytic systems will require more information than what is provided by your BPM transaction systems. Those systems extend your vision only as far as you and your partner agree. Retail customers such as Wal-Mart or Tesco can deliver near real-time point-of-sale information, from their cash registers, to selected partners in their networks. In other situations, a supplier may know little more than goods were received at the retailer's distribution center. Without a clear picture of what is actually being consumed, safety stocks tend to be greater.

No matter how good your information about your processes, your business also needs information about market trends, your customers, and your markets that comes from third-party providers such as AC Nielsen and IMS Health. This third-party information is often difficult to integrate with your data and so is out of date by the time you access it. BPM technologies such as Tilion and Unicorn will make it easier and faster for these companies to collect and publish data. In addition, trading hubs such as Covisent and Eurostar will use these technologies to produce analytic data as a value-added subscription service to businesses using their trading platform. Figure 7.5 calls attention to several analytics that are used to enhance business processing.

Analytics were once the ultimate strategic system, built in-house by your staff. This is still true in industries such as pharmaceuticals and financial services where knowledge of the business and the problems to be solved is as important as knowledge of computer science. Other

What Is It Called?	What Does It Do?
Supply chain network analysis	Provides analysis of the cost, profit, and service trade-offs in the supply chain for alternative sourcing, manufacturing, distribution, and transportation scenarios
Demand planning	Creates a demand forecast, aggregating information collected in collaboration with customers, suppliers, and channel partners
Inventory level management	Assesses the trade-offs among inventory levels, budget, and customer service
Marketing analytics	Assesses the effectiveness of your marketing campaigns; produces customer and customer-segment-specific analytics
Pricing and revenue optimization analytics	Assesses the impact of pricing decisions across contracts — useful when contracts are reintegrated; also uses point-of-sale data to fine-tune pricing at point-of-sale level

Figure 7.5   Analytics Enhanced with BPM (Source: CSC's Research Services)

industries are turning to packaged applications from vendors like i2, Siebel, and Manugistics that purport to provide a full suite of applications to link transactions and analytics in one expensive but comprehensive box. Market research companies such as AC Nielsen also offer specialized tools to perform analytic tasks based on their market research information such as category management and shelf space planning.

The build or buy debate pits speed to deployment against tools uniquely targeted to your business's strategy. Equally important, if no one in your business understands how the complex new analytics package works, then no one will use it, and costly mistakes will occur. The vendors appear to be considering unbundling their large applications in response to market pressure. Customers want to deploy one analytic capability at a time, and only with customers at the right level of supply chain maturity.

The key question becomes: How ready is a firm to progress to higher levels of supply chain maturity? With BPM, you and your partners will be deciding which role must be performed and how much information will be shared. Many of your existing partners will expect you to be an open public player in their supply chain and will ask: Are your processes and systems ready to share this information? Referring to Figure 7.6, which shows the five levels of supply chain evolution, that question

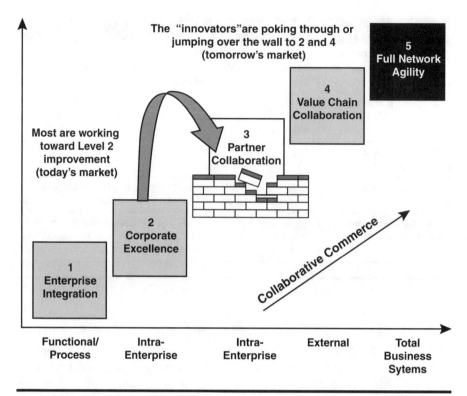

Figure 7.6 The Supply Chain Evolution

relates to determining the readiness to participate in levels 4 and 5, whether as a nucleus firm or a supporting partner.

The supply chain evolution and maturity model, as described in Figure 7.6, rates a business on the extent of visibility and control in its supply chain and on its ability to customize its processes for each customer. What level your firm has attained is a critical question to answer before embarking on the sharing of analytics between enterprises. Large nucleus firms are showing ever-greater impatience with partners asking for preferred positions and not having the capability to actively participate in e-business sharing at the network level and help with the desired customization features. Often these firms turn to some form of pilot test to select the long-term partners. Prototyping often has been used as a technique in determining capabilities, but BPM introduces yet one more feature that supersedes this usually slow process.

Simulations Will Replace Prototyping for Process Discovery, Design, and Analysis

Before BPM, prototypes often were used to test user interface of new processes but seldom were capable of proving that the process would meet performance goals. Performance verification came late in the development cycle, sometimes with unwelcome surprises.

The new BPM approach will use process definitions as a basis for process and business simulation, to dramatically shorten and de-risk the change life cycle. Figure 7.7 displays an outline of this new model for supply chain agility, which firms such as IDS Scheer, Intalio, CSC, Lanner, and Popkin are developing now.

The overarching issue is how to maximize the benefit of the supply chain agility that BPM offers. Figure 7.7 illustrates the concept. A continuous cycle of business change begins with identification of the business issue. An example is reducing lost sales due to stock-outs during promotions while maintaining lean inventories in the supply chain. The next link in the cycle is to evaluate the process alternatives available,

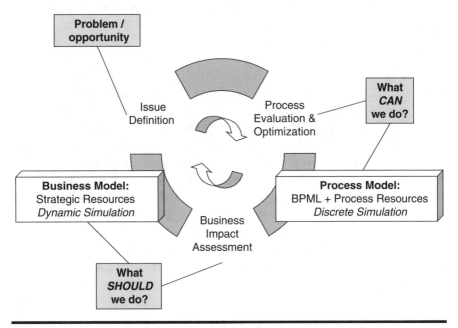

Figure 7.7 New Model for Supply Chain Agility

taking into account the resources that are or could be made available to support the processes. If 500 trucks are available and getting more is out of the question, then this is a constraint that must be factored in. Similarly, if your technology delivers sales information with a two-day delay, but a possible element of the solution space is new technology (at a price!) that will deliver sales information within one hour, then these alternatives must be evaluated. Discrete simulation tools such as Lanner Witness make it possible and convenient to explore complex process and resource scenarios, and in the future all successful supply chain businesses will rely on such tools to secure and hold advantage.

The final element of the cycle is the business simulation. Changing your supply chain processes, resources, and IT will still involve cost and risk, and therefore it will be essential to have the highest possible confidence that the business outcome will be what is desired. Systems dynamics is the best available technology here, as promoted by leading research institutions such as MIT and London Business School. Systems dynamics models do not guarantee the outcome you expect — nothing can in an unpredictable world — but they raise the likelihood considerably.

One note of caution is worth sounding here — To build a high-quality process and business models, you will need two things: high-quality attention from your top people and analysts with considerable depth of training and experience.

With BPM, no one loses sight of the metrics a business process is to achieve. Process design is a joint operation between business and IT, involving all the key players in a process. Process simulation tools such as those developed by Lanner that have enabled firms such as Campbell, Diagio, and Lucent to validate their processes before deployment are now linked to BPM systems. The major process modeling tool vendors such as IDS Scheer also provide a simulation capability. The tool that is used to develop the metrics also develops the process design. The design team establishes a set of target metrics and then modifies the process design until the metrics are achieved. The team can also validate a current process by assessing existing process designs. There are no more endless arguments over problem sources and solutions when you can view the process in operation. As importantly, the process simulated is the one actually deployed — since the process language such as BPML is used to share languages between the simulator and the BPMS that deploys the process. To illustrate this contention, let's consider the logistics company of the future, as depicted in Figure 7.8.

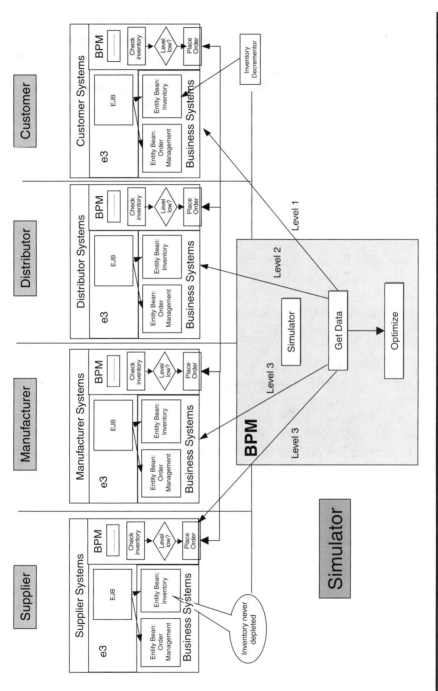

Figure 7.8 With Simulation, Supply Chain Strategy Design Can Be Tested Before Deployment (Source: CSC's Research Services)

A leading European logistics company believes that process simulations will both improve its competitive advantage and enhance the family life of its account executives. Today, its account executives get up early in the morning and check their computer systems to be ready to discuss problems, such as delayed shipments in any one of dozens of major hot spots around the globe. This means they know about problems before their customers call and can have a solution ready. While the customer is impressed that the logistics company is aware of and already working on the issue, and may even be convinced that the root cause of the problem was its own error and not a delivery problem, the company is not entirely satisfied. Packages are still late, and someone must assume the cost of lost time while a production line waits for critical parts.

CSC and Lanner, a business process technology company, have used integrated simulation with BPMS design and deployment tools. A customer firm can come to the CSC lab and simulate a process and then deploy it using BPM.

The real tragedy of this situation is that the delivery firm knows its customers, its suppliers, and the delivery routes so well that it can design a logistics process that can avoid these kinds of problems. In a future environment, this logistics company plans to use its knowledge to take over the logistics planning for its customers. It will use a simulation to demonstrate to its customers why some scenarios will result in delays and why the planning and routing it proposes will result in on-time and on-cost delivery. It will then use BPM to manage the logistics process and to optimize the process as its customers' needs change. As importantly, key executives will have more time with their families, because they will no longer need to spend the early mornings getting ready for meetings with dissatisfied customers.

The key to this new method of designing processes is the process simulator, which includes the discovery, design, optimization, and analysis capabilities of BPM software. This simulator is not tied to a fixed location. Management teams can use it in any conference room and support team members at remote locations. The simulator provides the business with a working model of the process, enabling a management team to understand the impact of proposed process changes on process metrics and on the IT systems and other resources used by the process. The business process simulator not only assesses a new business process design, but also shows what changes will be needed to the organization, staffing, IT systems, and data to put it in place. Because the simulator is part of a BPMS that can also deploy, execute, and operate processes, new processes can be quickly piloted and then implemented in accordance with governance procedures.

BPM also changes the beginning point of new process design, starting from nothing required to much reinvention of the routine. Starting from an existing design, usually an established best practice from outside the organization, was better but still required the tedious translation of a paper design into specifications for changes to systems and data across all business partners. With BPM, best practices will be available in BPML (or an industry-appropriate version of a business process management language). Every business will have a business process repository. In addition, a Napster-like technology will locate relevant process packs and then tailor the collected business process to a customer's specific requirements. Business partners will come to a process design meeting with several alternative methods for combining capabilities to provide the same business process. During simulation, the business will decide whether to use an existing business process or to invent a new one. Once a new one is invented, it is stored in a process repository and can be reused when appropriate.

BPM's sequence of simulate, test, then "make it so" also makes it easier to change a process once a problem is found. Therefore, expect frequent, incremental changes as well as major process redesign efforts. Supply chain teams may come to the business process simulation center for monthly or bimonthly reviews to assess process performance and assess alternative process designs. During a crisis such as a dock strike or a plant fire, the process simulation center will help the business, its customers, and other partners develop and deploy an alternative process.

Empowered People Will Be a Reality, Not a Slogan

As firms come together in the networks, the real beneficiaries will be the people doing the work that makes sense of all the effort. Thanks to BPM, machines will take over many tasks that people now do. Financial information, for example, can be gathered in real time if the relevant systems are properly integrated. Cisco already claims to be capable of closing its books every night. The focus now shifts to what can be learned from the figures and how managers should respond. As BPM reduces the time and cost required in automating processes, expect to see more and more automation. Machines will take over the once people-intensive jobs of locating (or filing) information in different systems, transferring information from one system (or company) to another, or making decisions based upon complex but well-defined rules.

Therefore, organizations will need fewer people, and those people will have jobs very different from those they have today. Whether they are in manufacturing, at the shop counter, or in the research and development laboratory, people will be reserved for activities such as problem solving, case work, innovation, and sense making. They will need a wealth of information and the tools to analyze that information and will expect access to the tools to do their job on the job site, at the customer site, and even at home. They will work in teams, with customers and other partners, and require support for complex team activities that cross business boundaries.

In the networked enterprise, people — not machines — will drive process innovation. A BPMS will make sure that process breakdowns do not go undetected; people will solve the customer's problem. Murphy's Law ("If something can go wrong, it will") and its various extensions ("If something can't go wrong, it will" and "If two things can go wrong, they will — in the worst possible order") should be the guiding principle of anyone setting up an automated process. New processes, like unreliable machinery, need constant monitoring and oversight. As our confidence increases, we tend to leave them to run unattended, but only if we can be sure that we will be alerted when something goes wrong. At that point, a human being will need to make a decision.

In the early days of the automobile, cars used to sport pressure gauges on the top of the radiator so the driver could monitor them constantly. Nowadays, we are so confident of radiator and hose technology that many cars have nothing but a little red light to indicate that the engine temperature is too high. We take the cooling system of the engine for granted, but we still like to be warned when it fails so that we can stop at a convenient place rather than ruin the engine. In the business world, many unusual situations can be predicted and handled automatically; in effect, they can be absorbed into the main process. Attention will focus on the system crashes, the multiple failures, and so forth that require the intervention of a skilled human. Computers should support this intervention by providing diagnostic information, tools for analysis and simulation, and, as far as possible, logic and rules that will still prevent illogical and dangerous interventions.

People, not systems, learn and innovate. That becomes the essential element for enhancing business performance. Machines can store and process information, but they cannot see significance in it. It takes humans in call centers, field services organizations, and research and development organizations to spot new patterns, to abstract common themes from different situations, to learn lessons. As the routine activity of business becomes seamlessly integrated and automated, every transaction will record itself in a standard format and be available for analysis.

Creative collaboration will increase within and across businesses as the network expands. In the past, creative collaboration was limited to special projects, where departments and business units of the same company or several companies agreed to field a multidisciplinary team to solve a specific problem or to design a new product. The most common method for managing such teams was to co-locate the team members in a common workspace and to provide a supportive collaborative environment. This way of supporting collaborative teams presumes they are relatively rare and once established will last long enough to warrant developing a separate workspace.

In the future, collaboration will be more ad hoc. Teams will form and dissolve around specific issues and problems. This will require new technologies for supporting collaboration when the team is not co-located. More importantly, two companies or business units must have an easy way to determine who is and who is not a team member with access to the team tools and information. In complex design activities, two methods are now used for managing what are called coupled activities: multidimensional problems with mutual dependencies. It is hard to design a gearbox, for example, if you don't know what the engine is going to be like. Similarly, it is hard to design an engine if you don't know anything about the gearbox that it has to drive. Designing gearboxes is a different discipline than designing engines, but some of the key decisions cannot be separated in the same way. The decision structure does not match the capability or knowledge structure.

The first method for managing coupled activities is to iterate toward an optimum solution. One side takes a stab at finding an answer, the other side modifies the solution to suit its purpose, and they throw it backward and forward until both parties are satisfied. The second is to reorganize the decisions so that the two disciplines focus first on the areas of interaction. It may be possible to agree first on the design of the interface between the engine and the gearbox. This will include shapes, strengths, tolerances, and the method of assembling them on the production line. Once done, the two sides are free to complete the rest of the design independently. This works well only if the design of the interface is not strongly dependent on any of the other design decisions they still have to make.

In the future, a third, more collaborative method will be used which draws the disciplines involved together into one team to tackle the whole design as a single problem. This third option is possible because of the visibility and control now available from BPM technology. Managers from both disciplines will know the state of the design and can be confident that they have the right copy of the design. This option can open up dramatic, innovative possibilities if the scope of the problem does not become overwhelming. The specific activities that are coupled together need to be identified and then brought together in the project plans so that they can be tackled by a joint team.

Conclusions

As firms move forward, they can decide to go beyond internal supply chain improvement and participate in an extended network for advanced capabilities. There are three paths available: as a nucleus firm acting with the help of a limited number of allies, for its own interests; as a nucleus firm assisting others to participate as willing and trusted partners focused on a key business customer; or as a supplier, enabler, distributor, or other node on the nucleus firm's activities. In the most advanced case, such a network will focus with the help of a major business customer on end consumer demand and supply solutions better than any competing group.

In each instance, BPM becomes the enabling mechanism for the critical information transfer that brings optimization to the processing that must take place. Many examples have been given of how BPM enhancement comes in many different flavors. As you consider the supply chain evolution of your firm, it becomes important to determine which route you wish to pursue on your way to being part of a networked enterprise. We close this chapter with one final note: If you don't do it, your competitor will.

8

ELIMINATE THE DRUDGERY AND EMPOWER THE PEOPLE

At this point, you might be somewhat convinced that business process management (BPM) provides the technical capability to better manage the rapid design and deployment of networked supply chains. However, you may still doubt the practical reality of getting even a small group of different business firms to agree on a set of common processes. This skepticism is probably grounded in a previous bitter experience with reengineering efforts in your own company, in attempting to adopt industry best-practice programs, or in the results of trying a slew of e-commerce initiatives.

Our experience indicates you should expect resistance — from your management, your customers, your suppliers, and other stakeholders. These constituents have been promised a networked supply chain before, usually powered by technology represented by three-letter acronyms (ERP, SRM, and CRM come to mind). You will need to convince these constituents that this approach to building a networked enterprise is different, and then deliver the business results you promise. This challenge means constructing an effective network and delivering better business metrics, while creating the skills you and your partners need to deepen collaborative partnerships. It also means you have found the secrets to eliminating most of the drudgery involved in data processing and interenterprise communication and have empowered the people performing the work to select and use appropriate information on a real-time basis.

This chapter shows how BPM provides an entirely new approach to process design and implementation, one that is particularly adept at addressing the issues of deployment across business boundaries and at aiding people in their search for helpful knowledge. It also provides proven techniques to manage BPM projects to success. In particular, we will present examples of how firms such as Norwich Union used BPM to reduce costs and speed up work by allowing a business process management system (BPMS) to do work once done by people. The people are happier since they no longer are performing tedious, time-consuming chores better accomplished by computer. Making that type of implementation a success begins with careful selection of where to start.

Pick the Right Target to Begin

A networked supply chain should be created to deliver superior business results to a specific customer or consumer segment, as well as to each of the constituents adding value in the supply chain. Therefore, you are well advised to select an opening project for which the implementation of some level of shared processes will deliver significantly better business results — in terms of quality, time to market, lower costs, or some other measure important to your firm and your customers. This project should also prove conclusively that the people doing the implementation have found their tasks less onerous and are excited about being able to direct their part of the interactions in a more positive manner. From a practical viewpoint, when selecting a first project, pick one that can be implemented in under six months and have payback in less than a year. This generally means that the project can be implemented using BPM with existing information technology (IT) investments and that some basics of a common trading vocabulary or ontology exist with the intended partners.

To eliminate drudgery and improve supply network operations, many businesses have begun their initial efforts by focusing on:

■ Automating ordering, invoicing, and payment for existing contracts between existing customers, suppliers, and other partners, thereby eliminating the costs and tediousness of processing paper invoices.

■ Developing explicit measurements for processes across the supply network and sharing process metrics such as work in progress, quality, availability to ship, or other process metrics with key suppliers and customers to shorten cycle times. This technique enables each member of the network to better respond to market conditions.

■ Developing shared processes that allow each member of the network to share customer information, sales backlogs, and results of customer surveys. This allows the firms to work together and build better solutions and a more customer-centric system of response, while aiding those in the planning area to develop more meaningful schedules and responses.

■ Deploying processes for automating the dissemination of technical information to customers and suppliers for earlier involvement in product design and delivery, while assisting those doing the designs to get the kind of help they need to dramatically shrink cycle times.

The linked firms then move into advanced improvements, typically in purchasing, procurement, and strategic sourcing, where BPM helps facilitate the processing using trusted external sources to add value to an initial list of mutually beneficial action items. This step could include a form of supplier relationship management with a few key suppliers to prove the value of having these suppliers play a greater role in strategy, planning, and execution of the business plan. Next, they tackle all of the logistics issues surrounding inbound and outbound shipments, warehousing and inventory management, and the efficiency of getting products and services delivered on time in a manner suitable to the most important customers. Advanced supply chain management efforts then focus on the details of greater collaboration and delve into customer relationship management, collaborative design and development, and collaborative planning, forecasting, and replenishment.

Many firms have a long list of quick hits that have languished on the shelf simply because past technology could not deliver the process and projects in a time and cost that made business sense. As failure to implement was recognized, the people involved lost faith in the ability of the supply chain to move beyond level 2 in the progression. The speed and low cost of BPM now make many of these projects viable and can re-energize the people into action. If your business does not have such a list, then pull together a group of customers and suppliers for a partnering diagnostic laboratory, a proven technique that involves a one-day planning session and a two-day workshop to identify quick hits. This technique will be described later in the chapter.

You want the first BPM implementation to kick-start the improvement by delighting business managers and equipping the implementers with a platform of new skills. The ideal project is highly visible, addresses something of real importance to the business and the people, hits the right level of risk for your business culture, and provides a convincing demonstration of BPM by achieving something that other technologies could not. The two key parameters are the process sector within the supply chain to be addressed and the scope of the process to be redesigned and better managed. The choice depends on your business's needs, the scale of investment available, and your appetite for risk and benefit. We suggest selecting from a prioritized short list of opportunities, some of which have been languishing and some of which will meet current market needs.

Choose an Approach That Fits the Process Experience and Culture of Your Firm

Once you have picked a target, you can take either of two approaches to execution. The first approach is to simply sit down with selected key customers and partners, get their agreement on the importance of the area to be improved, and begin to design and deploy, in a top-down manner, a new process that will be more effective. All participants should make contributions, drawing from their better results and applying BPM in a mutual manner to transfer the knowledge that will best suit the desired targeted changes. This may sound overwhelming, but with a top-down approach to process redesign it is actually the more straightforward way to begin. When you start with a group of experienced practitioners dedicated to making needed improvements, give them a tool that eliminates much of the difficulty in the processing, and keep the redesign simple, the complex becomes manageable.

The other way is to implement the detailed process designs, which you and your partners have tried to develop but have not been able to deploy, in a bottom-up manner. That means you gather the operators who are frustrated with the inefficiencies with a current process and allow them to recommend the means to make life easier for all parties. You should anticipate one area of concern with this approach. For anyone who has been involved in an effort to develop agreement between different businesses on the exchange of important information, the idea of a shared business process may seem either like a joke or a complete nightmare. Without the necessary authority to move things forward, some of these groups quickly become bogged down in their efforts because of uncertainties surrounding authorization. The means to establish the parameters within which the groups can function and what data can be shared must be addressed before beginning this approach. Then the teams begin to think of processes as detailed descriptions of how people perform necessary work, and they turn their attention to eliminating the difficulties and finding the better methods.

The key issue in either approach is to establish who does what of importance. This starts by agreeing on what the overall shape of the existing "process" is from end to end and then who should perform which redesigned steps in the process. After that, the parties need to agree on the handover points, that is, what is necessary to complete each activity and what is going to be passed over to start the next step in the process. Once this "public interface" is accepted and each party has a working implementation of its own pieces, you have a working shared process. As the people find that they can get better results with less effort, the enthusiasm to go further generally accelerates.

This simple level of agreement is all that is required to begin the process redesign, but other issues will rapidly arise. BPM provides a way to handle some of the most important ones. Visibility typically becomes the next expected issue, as people want to see what is happening and gain access to previously sacrosanct information that could be useful in their part of the processing. A basic principle helps move the constituents through this area. Each party can keep control of its own way of working, as long as it conforms to the basic agreement to redesign and improve the work.

In concept, each constituent could keep its internal processes entirely secret, but in practice much of the advantage of shared process management comes from being able to look into carefully selected parts of your partners' business activities. Therefore, there must be elements of mutual sharing at work in order for the effort to succeed, and the areas of acceptable knowledge exchange should be part of an up-front agreement. Logistics companies, for example, allow their customers to see how their packages have progressed in the shipment process. If the involved partners were using BPMS to manage their internal processes, then the same visibility (if the parties agreed) could be applied to any thread of business activity.

The final issue is validation. It is easy to provide visibility without surrendering control of your internal processes, but there may be good reasons for doing exactly that in particular areas of the relationship. Many businesses have to guarantee that their activities are conducted in a certain way (pharmaceuticals and financial services, for example), and others may well want to build the same kind of assurances into their agreements with partners. BPM allows you the ability to publish the process you are actually using at whatever level of detail required. It thus offers a way of handling some complex issues of collaborative working, but it also allows the participating parties an opportunity to take these issues apart and reassemble them for best overall advantage.

Redesign Your Existing Process, But Don't Be Afraid to Build Upon Your Extensive Backlog of Unimplemented Process Designs

With these parameters in place, we recommend the following steps for achieving the greatest benefits from your first targets.

Begin with discovery and design, if you are either very poor or very good at process thinking. Businesses new to process thinking, or those that have not yet applied process thinking in the chosen business area, need a discovery and design approach to better understand and define the process steps involved and to get people working together for mutual benefit. For example, consider a nucleus firm and its business suppliers that have just begun to work cooperatively. A discovery project is often useful in building a common understanding of the reality that forms the basis for discovery of a new and improved business procedure that helps each partner. In many businesses, senior management beliefs about how the market and the linked businesses operate are very different from the way they actually operate.

When you bring many businesses together, you are faced with even larger differences between how the end customer and the management of each business in the supply chain believes the supply chains functions. With a discovery tool, you can quickly show each business where management beliefs about how the business operates diverge from day-to-day operational reality. You can then also show how that reality does or does not conform to customer expectations. You next begin the planning process with a common understanding of customer expectations and a clearer appreciation for how the business may change its processes to better meet those expectations.

At the other extreme, businesses used to process improvement programs, such as Six Sigma quality, are finding it more difficult to reach continuous improvement goals. The volume of process information makes it difficult to identify specific targets of opportunity for achieving added value. The new generation of business process discovery and design tools accelerate that part of supply chain processing significantly.

Firms that play an enabler role in logistics, warehousing, and supply chain management, for example, will use discovery tools when they work with their customers to assess their current paths to market and to quickly identify steps in the process where they can add value. These firms do so by suggesting new routes, new packing or warehousing techniques, or new local contacts to handle local practices such as customs and freight forwarding.

Next, start using new BPM tools where and when you are ready to deploy new processes or to modify existing processes. Many businesses have a backlog of process projects within their organization or across their network value chain. The customer service organization wants to provide customers with the ability to place orders and check order status on-line, senior management wants to quickly integrate a new acquisition into the business, manufacturing wants to create more flexible schedules, and so on. Any of these projects offers the opportunity to acquire a BPM platform and to build the skills and experience you need to be a process-focused business. The project you choose and the rationale for selecting BPM technology depend on the types of problems facing your business and the willingness of your key executives to engage in process thinking. A few parameters in selecting from your short list apply:

- Choose systems integration projects if you are facing a backlog of such projects due to a recent merger or acquisition or need to integrate an enterprise resource planning (ERP) system with bolt-on or legacy applications. This will reduce the time and cost of systems integration while building your understanding of BPM technologies. You also gain the power of BPM to design and deploy the process and to change it. The caution is to avoid BPM being viewed as an IT project and not getting the business fully involved in process redesign.

- Choose a business process implementation project if you are facing a backlog of requests from the business units to implement processes that span applications and/or business boundaries. Where process thinking is ingrained in both the business and IT, BPM technology provides an environment where they can work together. The drawback for a first project is the inherent risk of deploying any technology for the first time in a project with high visibility.

If you do not fall into either of these categories, the best approach may be to watch and wait. Your current enterprise application integration efforts, use of middleware, and/or workflow vendors may provide you with BPM tools as you upgrade software. Equally important, you can learn by watching what others are doing. Alternatively, actively seek out a business unit manager with a business issue best supported by BPM and run a pilot project that solves the problem, provides a proof of concept for BPM technology, and instills the business and its IT group with the skills and experience to handle further projects. The chief limitation of this approach is that pilot projects are often small and the results are not fully accepted by the business.

If that is the case, you should then carefully choose a BPM technology that provides the capabilities needed to resolve the business problems you have chosen to address. BPM is a relatively new technology, and you cannot yet buy an integrated BPMS from a single vendor that provides all eight of the capabilities defined by the Business Process Management Initiative. You should not be deterred by this limitation. At any point in time, a process improvement program is unlikely to need all eight of these capabilities, particularly at the start. As with any product selection, you simply need to match the business requirements with the product's capabilities. The choice of BPMS will center on factors such as the nature of the process that you want to integrate, the extent to which you want to manage your process across business boundaries, and the extent to which you want to leverage an existing technology infrastructure, including applications, middleware, and transaction monitors.

Start Using BPM When Ready to Deploy or Modify Processes

In many supply networks, you do not need to begin with discovery. If the key players have worked together before and are using BPM to deploy a process that has been poorly supported by older technology, you can begin using the process design tools provided by the suppliers of BPMS tools. These tools are organized around a design console, used by the process designer to create the process model. Once the model is established, the process designer then decides how the model will interface with process participants — systems, people, and other businesses. He or she then browses the set of available participants and attaches the appropriate one to the model. Once the designer and the relevant business partners decide that the process model is complete, they are a click away from deployment. The BPMS handles communication among systems, people, and other businesses for all constituents. Together, they choose a BPM technology that provides the capabilities needed to resolve the business problems the partners have chosen to address.

The biggest issue you will face with BPM tools is your choice of business process modeling language. Soon you will be able to buy tools that come with standards such as the Business Process Modeling Language (BPML), configured for your specific industry. Today, you will find that only a few of the 160 software vendors that support the BPML standard actually use BPML. Many still apply a preparatory version of a business process modeling language. This situation will not hinder your ability to get started managing the redesign across your supply chain, but it will limit the degree of visibility and control you have with partners that do not have the same BPMS.

For supply chain applications, standard-based tools are preferable. However, in many industries, such as telecommunications, oil, and financial services, proprietary tools are already widely used, which makes collaboration across business boundaries fairly straightforward without use of a standard-based BPMS. In those situations, the designers can figure on deployment of proprietary BPMS (e.g., Fuego in telecommunications and oil and Clear I in insurance).

Another caveat is in order:, BPM technology is not enough. Building BPM competency requires understanding, targets, and skills. Implementing BPM technology will not make your business process competent. Achieving process competency requires a sound understanding among senior managers of its importance and potential for the business, clear targets from strategists who define precisely how it is going to be exploited, and a rich set of skills among the implementers that enables them to do the job effectively and efficiently. These three requirements interact and reinforce each other; thus, they have to be developed together.

It is also necessary to cultivate demand for a supply chain network powered by BPM through education of your executive team regarding the advantages to be gained. First, create awareness of the new possibilities in your executive team. Don't expect to get by with a general education program. You will need to prove that BPM will solve long-standing issues in your business or provide new enhancement opportunities. Many businesses have adopted the CSC's Research Services Innovation framework as an educational tool. This five-step framework includes:

- **The supply**: What are the new BPM componentized architectures and new data integration tools? How have they been successfully applied to build networked supply chains? When answering these questions, assemble concrete case studies and demonstrations.
- **The demand**: How can you apply BPM to provide greater visibility and control across your supply chain? *This needs to be tied to a transaction, process, and collaboration framework.* What are the benefits to your customers, suppliers, and other partners? How has BPM changed the time scale and/or price tag for meeting these demands?
- **The risks**: What are the risks, including lack of effective project management, of applying BPM? Just as important, what are the risks of continuing to use older technologies if your competitors or customers adopt BPM?
- **The connectors**: What common threads in demand do you see across customers, suppliers, and the business? How can BPM projects be structured to take advantage of these connections to spread infrastructure investment costs across business units with similar needs?
- **The approach**: What are the business interests of each stakeholder? How can you craft a business case that addresses the concerns of each stakeholder?

Then you need to educate your customers and partners. Once you build consensus in your business that BPM will enable you to quickly deploy a networked supply chain, your next task will be to continue the same process with your customers and partners. Again, expect an initial reaction of skepticism, in part because they have heard much of this before. Suppliers may have genuine concerns that the proposed supply chain project is no more than one more effort to force them to lower costs without delivering costs savings to their business. In many cases, past supply chain integration projects have actually increased their cost base because they have had to invest in expensive technology for that specific project. Customers will be skeptical that any new collaboration is just an effort to up sales or cross-sell additional products without delivering any new value to their clients. Therefore, you need to market each and every proposed project to each and every customer and supplier. Figure 8.1 shows a matrix of the kinds of questions typically encountered as groups work interactively to define improved processing across a networked enterprise.

For initial projects or pilots, you should expect that neither the business nor IT group is ready for interenterprise process management. This means that you should plan to build new skills as you deploy BPM. BPM sets a new standard for business in almost any industry. Neither your business nor IT is likely to have the full range of necessary skills. You may find the key skills in consultants or in partners, but you must understand what skills you need and how they can be developed. Teach the skills that are easily taught, and recruit for the skills more closely tied to personality type and acquired through varied career experience. Above all, keep the objective of removing the drudgery and empowering the people with new abilities at the forefront of the effort.

Process management requires three distinct categories of skills:*

A. **Applied skills** or subject matter expertise is knowledge about how to do things, generally demonstrated by an ability to complete a specific task. Skills are found in practitioners, not managers. IT staff can learn applied skills through training and mentoring, but it may be harder to build new applied business skills that require specific knowledge about why a process is done the way it is.

B. **Behavioral skills**, including communication, collaboration, persuasion, education, and leadership, take time to acquire. In many

---

* For a more detailed discussion of the A, B, C skill framework, see Après le Déluge — Post-Y2K Staffing Problems, *Foundation Research Journal*, March 2000.

INNOVATION ISSUES: KEY QUESTIONS

THE SUPPLY

- Do you make sure that you are aware of the changes in technologies and that you understand when they become appropriate to use in your business or in the creation of entirely new businesses within your firm?
- Do you take advantage of the knowledge of partners, vendors, and consulting firms to augment your own understanding?
- Do you hear regularly from the mavericks in your own organization?
- Is your organization prepared to take advantage of technologies when they hit a threshold in price or performance (for example, when wireless data transmission to laptops and personal digital assistants achieves both high speed and broad coverage)?

Example: Awareness of developing technologies led one defense contractor to deploy key elements of a scalable infrastructure that supports rapid connection and co-working between organizational units, both within and outside the firm.

THE DEMAND

- Do you know what others in the business are thinking about in terms of new offerings, new business combinations, and new lines of business?
- Do you know the instances in which IT is thought to be the barrier to new business?
- Do you understand how to match the capabilities of new technologies with the demands of the rest of the business so that you avoid the appearance of just pushing technology?
- Are you prepared for spikes in the demand for new capabilities?
- Do you manage the demand by educating the rest of the business about possibilities that new technologies create, without overpromising?

Example: At an aerospace firm this meant assigning technology-savvy consultants to coach the senior directors for six months. At a transportation firm this meant providing top management every week with 15 selected articles from the technology and business literature.

THE RISKS

- Do you explicitly manage and overcome both the traditional risks of any new project as well as the extra risks that are often attributed to innovative projects?
- Do you make explicit the risks of not pursuing an innovation?
- Do you make it clear in advance to the rest of the business that it is likely to get worse before it gets better (for example, in the case of an ERP implementation)?
- Do you actively watch for signs of MEGO (My Eyes Glaze Over, a feeling often expressed by the rest of the business in response to an IT presentation) in your interactions with the rest of the business?

Figure 8.1 The Key Questions to Ask for BPM Implementation (Source: CSC's Research Services)

- Do you insist that communicating with people is one of the key tasks on which your IT team will be judged?
- Do you provide a mechanism by which the innovation team can share in the success of the innovation?

Example: Most start-up companies and new spin-offs of existing companies use an equity stake in the new company as a way to engage the staff in actively managing and overcoming risk.

THE CONNECTIONS

- Do you look beyond simply matching the immediate supply and demand?
- Do you make sure that you have taken a sufficiently abstract view so that you see the connections to other nearby opportunities?
- Do you see the connections between your work and that of others in the firm?

Example: A manufacturing firm that was trying to reduce the length of time needed for government approval of its products realized that the same process could be used by other parts of the business to reduce time to market in general. The trick was to take a view of the innovation that obstructed the key elements and then look for how it would fit with other problems.

THE APPROACH

- Having correctly seen the demand, supply, risks, and connections, have you explicitly decided what is the best way to carry out the innovation?
- Do you have an explicit plan for what, when, and how you should let others in the organization know about your efforts?
- Do you understand the culture of the organization? Innovating through technology can take many forms. Which is the best for your culture?
- Do you understand where the business stands financially? It may be easiest to seek innovations when things are either very bad or very good. In between, there may be strong pressure to just cut costs and be more efficient at doing what you are doing now.
- Can you see beyond your garden wall? Do you understand partnerships and virtual companies?

Example: A global transportation firm now makes a determination of the right approach for each technology-driven innovation. Should it be a leadership project, in which the firm takes primary responsibility for designing, crafting, and implementing the innovation? Should it be a partnership project, where responsibility is shared, both within and outside the organization? Or should it be a project where the role of the firm is to watch carefully until a technology or capability is sufficiently mature and then move quickly to deploy it?

Figure 8.1 The Key Questions to Ask for BPM Implementation (continued)

organizations, they are found in the business but not in IT. Look for translators who can bridge this gap, and use specialized training courses and consultancies, but do not expect rapid changes if the business culture and reward systems have not fostered them in the past.

C. **Cognitive skills,** such as sense making, creativity, and systems thinking, are needed to create new solutions. These skills are the most difficult to learn and are key to your success. In many cases, IT, rather than the business, has the required cognitive skills to make sense of and to develop systematic responses for what may appear to be chaotic, conflicting demands from customers, suppliers, and other partners.

These are the critical skills of the business, process, and technical architects. Because it is easier and faster to choose a team that already has the required C skills than it is to develop them, you may have to recruit or use some consultants. The technical architect may be the easiest role to fill. For example, the architect of your middleware strategy could also master the BPM architecture. Business and process architects could be developed by having IT professionals with the requisite C skills work closely with a process owner from the business and in time be assigned to the business rather than IT.

IT must be part of the core team in this round of reengineering. BPM will require a deeper, more creative partnership between the organization and IT than exists in most businesses. The process owner must be a senior manager based in the business, but the business cannot design processes alone and then expect IT to choose the right applications and infrastructure to implement them. Business and IT must combine their expertise with a thorough understanding of the new agility and transparency that BPM provides. This up-front integration of business and IT will deliver the fastest business results. IT must participate fully in creative collaboration as new processes evolve.

When selecting a team, make sure you include people with the right mix of B and C skills, as shown in Figure 8.2. A skills are also needed, but you can more easily acquire these skills through training. Mark Evans, CIO of Tesoro Petroleum, believes that the new BPM tools will have a big impact on his IT organization. "In the future," he says, "the critical value that IT brings to the table will be through business process architects and project managers. All else becomes commodity IT and

Applied Skills	Behavioral Skills	Cognitive Skills
Consultation	Results orientation	Systems thinking
Systems integration	Risk tolerance	Process thinking
Prototyping	Resourcefulness	Abstraction
Modeling	Self-confidence	Invention
Simulation	Thoroughness and follow-through	Logic
Project management	Versatility	Lateral thinking
Business knowledge	High energy	Pattern recognition
Technical fluency	Collaboration	Synthesis
	Humility	Curiosity
	Articulateness	Anticipation
When selecting a team, make sure you include people with the right mix of B and C skills. A skills are also needed, but you can more easily acquire these skills through training.		

Figure 8.2 Skills Needed for Effective Team Building

could be outsourced. Today, however, business process architects who can speak to the business and make creative use of the new BPM technologies are scarce." Mark believes that an important part of his job as chief information officer will be to develop these new business process architects through his leadership and the example that he sets.

Partnering Diagnostic Labs Help Establish the Right Operating Parameters

A technique mentioned earlier, which has proven to be very useful in finding hidden values within business relationships and determining how technology should be applied in a networked environment, is termed a partnering diagnostic laboratory (PDL). PDL has proven to be one of the most effective tools we have applied to help firms get started on collaboration and the mutual use of technology. A PDL is a simple but very powerful means of bringing partners together to analyze their relationship and to discuss the steps necessary between them to satisfy the ultimate network customer or consumer group. Having applied this technique with dozens of companies in many industries, we can say that it has never failed to improve the relationship and bring attention to values not normally developed in the general course of discussion. It has always resulted in the introduction of actions that enhanced the supply chain network and returned far more than the investment in the effort. Figure 8.3 illustrates the technique being considered.

The PDL provides a focused workshop environment to identify and prioritize opportunities that bring increased value to supply chain constituents. It is designed to be a simple means of bringing business partners together, either suppliers and manufacturers, manufacturers and distributors, manufacturers and customers, or any combination of firms in a value chain network that want to enhance their processing and take advantage of BPM capabilities. It comes in two phases and begins with a planning session, usually conducted with the nucleus firm acting as a sponsor for the effort. The objective is to develop ideas and concepts to be pursued in the PDL and to build the framework for future collaboration.

As part of the planning phase, the technique is fully discussed with the parties involved, several executives are interviewed to get their perspectives on how the relationship might be enhanced, and a set of preworkshop hypotheses is developed. This one-day activity focuses first with the sponsor on what the expected results should be and, in particular, which firm is an appropriate candidate for the PDL. Selection is done best with outside help to make certain the firm meets some predetermined criteria for useful participation, so as to ensure that the first effort is a success.

With such a partner, attention will be focused on how to develop ideas based on mutual best practices and how to consider specific internal and external industry practices which could be helpful. The intent is to achieve extra value in such areas as cycle time reduction, pooling of purchases, transaction costs, reducing dependency on safety stocks, better inventory management, interenterprise communication systems based on BPM, better asset utilization, and on-line visibility of data. A decision is then made whether or not to have a preliminary meeting with the selected partner. Most nucleus firms opt to have this additional session, so that the parties come prepared with a list of expectations from both sides and what the potential benefits for both companies might be.

With the partner selected, details are then worked out regarding how to create a simple but meaningful process map that shows the product, information, and financial flows between the organizations. The partners then determine the scope, purpose, details, and deliverables for the PDL. An effort to develop a preworkshop hypothesis (i.e., a statement of what improved set of conditions should be achieved) is included in this phase. Toward the end of the first session, a gap analysis is developed

Phase 1			Phase 2	
Potential Issues, Opportunities	**Proof of Concept**	**Process Review**	**Priority Actions Selected**	**Initiate Priority Actions**
Planning Session	*Initial Meeting*	*Go/No Go*	*Two-Day Work Session*	*Pilot Implementation*
• Review diagnostic tool	• Facilitate discussion	• Prepare workshop analysis	• Facilitate discussion	• Initiate top-priority action plans
• Interview executives	• Prepare letter to attendees	• Perform gap analysis	• Define character and scope	• Allocate resources
• Formulate pre-workshop hypothesis	• Commence pre-work	• Review improvement opportunities/ prioritize actions	• Describe execution model	• CSC monitors/ assists
• One-day review to agree on format, attendees, priorities, time schedule	• Discuss concepts	• Discuss cost - sharing ideas	• Prioritize action items	• Execute quick-hit opportunities
	• Process map		• Identify resources	• Evaluate
	• Generate ideas		• Prepare timetable	• Determine location, intended results
	• Prepare preliminary opportunities list		• Target results	• Initiate action plans
	• Identify top priorities		• Review procedures	• Track results
	• Identify benefits			

Figure 8.3 PDL Approach

to make a rough estimate of where the two firms might be in terms of significant measures. The idea is to get a feel for the potential benefits that could accrue. Then a decision is made as to whether or not to go forward, and a list of invitees and letter of invitation are developed.

In the second phase, a two-day diagnostic takes place. Now the objective is to develop mutually beneficial actions that will enhance interactive supply chain processes. The process map is fully discussed to make certain the important areas of interaction are included. The audience should include all pertinent functions from both partners. With consensus on the process flows, the group begins in earnest to consider all of the preliminary data from the planning session and begins constructing a straw man, or preliminary diagram, with ideas for an improved state of conditions. Brainstorming techniques are used to get active participation and generate ideas not normally considered by the parties.

Through several iterations, the activities continue until a preliminary list of improvement ideas has been generated, discussed, grouped into categories, and thoroughly evaluated. Typical items on such lists include establishing a better external communication system on-line, transferring knowledge to help each partner, shortening the cycle time from idea to approval, reducing logistics costs, cutting the need for inventory, finding short-term cost savings, and so forth. Now teams are formed to analyze the top five or six actions that might be taken. These groups report on what they believe to be the benefits of pursuing such efforts. When consensus is achieved on the very top actions, the activity moves to developing specific implementation plans, complete with action sponsor, scope of effort, required resources, preliminary action steps, timetable for execution, and order-of-magnitude costs and benefits.

Figure 8.4 depicts the kind of activities that have taken place. The actions are next arrayed on a matrix, usually broken out by time to implement and relative value of the effort. That means some sensible framework is used to set the actions into place by order of importance and priority. A final report and summary of activities is then prepared for management review. The deliverables include an outline of potential improvements and opportunities to enhance the relationship, a plan to validate the concepts and develop actual test results, and action team formation. With management support and endorsement of specific teams and actions, the effort proceeds and pilot efforts are initiated.

From previous efforts, the potential benefits include the means to:

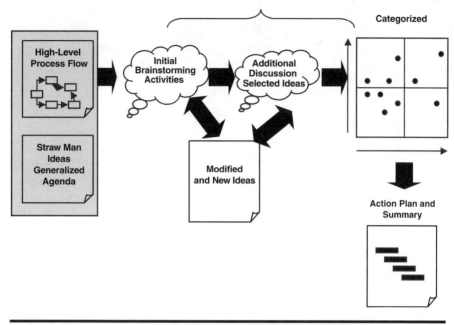

Figure 8.4 Generalized Approach for PDL Workshop

- Reduce errors in order processing
- Lower costs of procurement
- Reduce order fulfillment time and costs
- Shorten cycle time from order to delivery and order to cash
- Lower inventory and safety stocks
- Introduce new product more quickly and successfully
- Develop new and profitable revenues

Conclusions

In this chapter, we have illustrated an entirely new approach to business process design and implementation. Our techniques are intended to be more adept at addressing the issues of deployment across business boundaries and aiding people to access useful knowledge. Our advice is to select a likely project and use the steps and procedures outlined to achieve an early success and prove the value of the effort. Several alternative approaches were considered to offer the practitioner some options that better fit the actual company culture and environment.

9

GET STARTED BY ADDRESSING THE POINTS OF PAIN IN YOUR BUSINESS

Unlike older technologies, business process management (BPM) works well with your existing technologies to enhance business performance. Right from the start, the focus is on solving concrete business problems and laying a foundation for an ongoing process improvement program for your business and its key network partners. The hopeful element is that smart application of BPM can bring immediate solutions to today's business problems. There is an important concern, however, which must be considered.

Useful products are emerging in this brave new environment we are advocating, but the practitioner must be wary. Product introductions are developing rapidly, and there are still many uncertainties about the future shape of the market. In the long term, it is not even clear whether you will buy a dedicated business process management system (BPMS) or whether the process capability will be embedded in new releases of the products you already own. However, you can use BPM technologies now to meet business demands for complex integration with customers, suppliers, and other business partners. This chapter will explain how to introduce BPM by using it to solve today's points of pain, with demonstrably better results than older technology, and then expand the effort through a series of small successes into a full-blown BPM program.

First Choose a BPM Technology
That Provides Needed Capabilities

A firm should choose its BPM technology with both long- and short-term goals in mind. As you build your supply chain network, you will need all of the capabilities of BPM, from discovery to analysis. In many cases, your vendor selection will be based not only on technical capability but industry knowledge and experience within your industry. This chapter will provide some guidance in matching technology to your business needs.

In choosing BPM tools, remember that the power of the technology comes from the ability of the tools to share a common language for describing business processes. Therefore, we strongly suggest that you push technology vendors hard to support a single high-level standard for describing business processes. This approach will enable you to quickly and easily move process designs from a discovery and analysis tool to deployment and to simulate new process designs. More importantly, you and your trading partners will have full visibility and control of shared business processes without needing the same BPMS.

The current marketplace is divided into five categories. As a way of getting an initial handle on the different technologies available in this space, we suggest the following categorization:

1. **Discovery and design technologies**: These tools come from vendors whose roots lie in process modeling and design. They support the documentation of existing processes and the development and enhancement of new ones. Their real strength is in analyzing rather then simply displaying the process information, so they support the optimization of processes as well as the discovery and design features. The key differentiator between these tools is the extent to which the vendor plans to integrate them with other tools to provide for execution, interaction, and maintenance of the live process.
2. **Systems integration technologies**: These tools tend to come from vendors with an enterprise application integration, business-to-business, or middleware background. They bring a process per-

spective to systems integration tools, putting messages in the context of an overall process and managing that process from the outside. They provide a fast path to systems integration, but may be weaker on support for the kind of manual tasks that workflow customarily manages. They are not likely to be able to track execution of processes across business boundaries.

3 **Workflow-based technologies**: These tools focus primarily on helping human beings do their jobs — managing tasks, routing information, and providing on-line coaching. They provide better access to information in computer systems than traditional workflow, but are generally less capable when it comes to industrial-strength systems integration and automation.

4. **Best-of-breed process managers**: These offerings tend to come from system integrators, although some software vendors have developed commercial packages. They use a strong process methodology and a component-based architecture to combine workflow with systems integration capabilities. This approach significantly reduces the time and cost required to integrate business processes and provides a platform for rapid change within the enterprise. It is also a good way of building skills. Its principal limitation is that it will not readily support process collaboration across business boundaries.

5. **Purpose-built BPM**: These tools come from early-stage vendors or from systems integrators, and they come closest to fulfilling the definition of a complete BPM. They provide support for end-to-end process management, by taking a process design and using it to orchestrate other systems and human beings. They leverage rather then replace existing technology infrastructure. Within this category, there are important distinctions:

   a. *Proprietary tools*: These tools focus primarily on a specific set of issues within the business, between a business and its customers, or between a defined set of business partners. For example, one tool is strong on automating deterministic tasks once they are assigned to people, while another has a stronger track record in integrating enterprise resource planning (ERP), customer relationship management, and/or legacy systems. These tools tend to connect directly with the systems that support the process, and they may not, therefore, meet the needs of a fast-changing open business-to-business process where a looser coupling would be an advantage.

b. *Standards-based tools*: These tools are designed explicitly to use public infrastructure and to interoperate with tools from other vendors. Their great strength is that they will work easily, reliably and flexibly across business boundaries. The major limitation (at least for now) is that they are new and unproven. However, unlike ERP applications, they are well suited to proof-of-concept demonstrations and larger scale pilots.

As with any package selection, a firm is advised to balance long-term opportunities against short-term needs. It is very important to begin by defining your business requirements and then choose the appropriate tool. As with any emerging technology, it is equally important to balance long-term needs with immediate requirements. Keep in mind that all of these technologies will evolve and may catch up with long-term needs even if they don't meet them now. Ask vendors about their strategies, but don't bet the business on the answer they give you.

Rebuild the Business from the Outside In

With the technology selected, the firms then move to redesign, the building of improved systems and procedures, and the consideration of network construction. Managing a shared process with other companies will set the whole business in an entirely new perspective. Individual companies will no longer be seen as islands but rather as providers of capability to the extended enterprise. The correct advice is to begin the construction phase by looking at the linked businesses from the outside in. Activities once regarded as purely internal, especially problem solving and creative activities like production planning, creative product design, and business transformation, will be shared by networks of collaborating companies. This condition requires changes in your approach to governance, strategy, and business design, and both business and information technology (IT) will need to devote much more conscious attention to outside events — to sensing them, understanding and modeling them, and ultimately to shaping them. We are considering here the cultural vault to the external environment so important to advanced supply chain management techniques and results.

New issues will arise for business managers, and this fundamental change in the role of a business raises important issues for these managers. These issues include:

- **Legal issues**: The definition of an electronic contract and in particular the legal recognition of digital signatures and the governance standards that distinguish healthy collaboration from cartels and other unfair practices.

- **Information sharing**: Protocols for sharing information will have to include legally enforceable standards for the security and confidentiality of information revealed in the process of trading and clear rules for how information is returned when a relationship comes to an end.

- **Business model**: A collaborative business model will have to cover the costs of developing and operating the shared infrastructure and investments that benefit the enterprise as a whole, along with the fair allocation of profits.

- **Management structure**: Some aspects of the networked enterprise must be managed as a single entity, including the design, deployment, monitoring, and optimization of processes across the collaborative network.

- **Customer relationships**: How will customer service operate in a networked organization? How will brands be promoted, preserved, and protected? Who will "own" the customers, and who will benefit from getting closer to them? Can affordable and flexible mobile services be developed to enable customers to work anywhere, any time, using any device? How will accountability be ensured and customers protected when something goes wrong?

- **Collaboration and trading structures**: Evaluation of the strengths and weaknesses of existing collaborative structures, such as NetMarkets and industry hubs, and decisions about the role to be played in developing them. Analysis of the different costs, benefits, and risks of trading through private networked enterprises, industry hubs, or on public infrastructure.

New Issues Will Be Raised for the CIO and the IT Team

The role of the chief information officer (CIO) and the IT team in providing enabling technology will also be significantly changed. Issues in this area will include:

- IT people will collaborate much more with external parties. They will spend more time with customers, suppliers, and other partners negotiating interfaces that will work for everyone involved and making agreements about who will be responsible for providing what services.

- Processes will be invoked from outside. Routine processes such as ordering or payment may be called directly from the outside, either by collaborating businesses or by end customers. The implication is that the business will become more like a bundle of on-line services with "users" rather than "customers."

- Processes will be designed to fit into the bigger picture. The internal business processes must drive and respond to the broader cross-business processes that deliver value to the end customer. They must be designed to fit into the external processes smoothly, economically, and reliably.

- The information architecture (ontology) will be "socially defined." The content and meaning of the external messages that glue the networked enterprise together have to be agreed upon by the trading community. Internal systems must be capable of interpreting and processing this shared language (or languages).

- The technology that is deployed may need to be common. In some areas, exchange standards and message translation are unlikely to deliver the required robustness and flexibility; common technology may be the only answer. We expect this to be true particularly in the development and support of cross-business collaborative environments (including generic collaborative commerce technologies and complex and specialized collaborative planning and design tools).

Large Collaborative Projects Become Feasible

Advanced network partnering leads to many new opportunities. Your partnership with other businesses can enter a new phase of creative collaboration. The goal will be to create and to implement a truly digital business model. Participating firms must prepare to play their part, by providing the detailed technology planning and insight the linked businesses will need. You will increase your opportunities to help your business attain or maintain market leadership by steadily deploying technologies to work effectively in such a networked enterprise. Successful completion of large and complex projects in partnership with customers, competitors, and suppliers becomes possible, but will test your collaborative management skills to the limit.

BPM's critical success factors are simple and well understood, but difficult to achieve. After 20 years of improvement programs, there is little new to be said about the critical success factors. This list will be remarkably similar to any past list you have seen for other improvement programs. What is new is that the technical issues are receding. The technology vendor community is hard at work developing the tools you need to componentize your applications and to put them together to support the many ways your business wants to work. That leaves you free to concentrate on the more difficult cultural and organizational issues of developing a process-competent business. Figure 9.1 lists many of the factors involved in managing the change from the outside in. Then a ten-step procedure becomes helpful in successful execution.

1. Focus on Delivering Value —
One Customer or Customer Segment at a Time

Every round of process programs has stressed the importance of focusing in on the customer. Decide that it's time to do something better! Invest the time needed to understand your customers' business, their lifestyles, their markets, and their customers. Then, customize your processes for each customer or customer segment. Rethink segmentation strategies to identify those characteristics that help you choose the right capabilities for each customer. Work one on one with a few of your key customers to find new ways to drive out cost or time, to improve service, and/or to provide more customized solutions for them. This means eliminating work that does not add value, automating activities that can be fully specified, and empowering people with the tools and information to tackle the harder tasks of troubleshooting, decision making, innovation, and just getting to know your customers.

Within your business, the processes most likely to need improvement are those that are now people intensive: sales, marketing, research and development, and back-office functions such as claims processing and loan and credit approvals. Many theoretically automated activities now require people simply because they are poorly organized or require people to transfer or interpret information collected in different systems or departments. You need to give people the information and tools they need to do what they do best: talk to customers; make sense of complex,

	Outside In	Inside Out
Cultural Challenges	Develop cross-business collaborative mechanisms and protocols. ■ Assess the readiness of your industry for collaboration. (Have there been successful collaborative efforts in the past?) ■ Select one or more problems that can be successfully resolved through collaboration rather than competition. ■ Develop a clearly pre-scribed industry agenda to avoid antitrust issues. Articulate and enforce clear policies to enable trust between competitors. ■ Recruit a committed and focused management team with a track record that will win the trust of participants in the network.	Cultivate a willingness to listen to and depend upon partners, customers, suppliers, competitors, and enablers. ■ Choose one project to prove the concept of relying on external providers (success breeds success). ■ Train business and IT managers in the use of different types of partnership (contractual choice, coordinated co-working, creative collaboration). ■ Demonstrating management enthusiasm for offering services will help. Develop a willingness to trust competitors. ■ Demonstrate management focus on mutual benefit. ■ Articulate clearly bounded "zones" of collaboration. ■ Foster good personal relation-ships with many layers of management in customers, competitors, suppliers, and enablers.
Organizational Challenges	Select one or more industry problems that can be resolved by development of a net-worked enterprise. ■ Recruit a cross-enterprise team with industry knowl-edge and insight. ■ Recruit appropriate participants — customers, suppliers, competitors, enablers. ■ Define a business case for action. Verify that each participant perceives a clear business payoff from the proposed projects.	Identify your core capabilities. ■ Compare your business's capabilities with world and industry standards. ■ Determine what capabilities you will retain and may offer to others. ■ Determine what capabilities partners will provide. ■ Identify possible partners — customers, competitors, suppliers, and enablers. Map the value chains in which your business participates. ■ Identify problems and opportuni-ties in the value chain.

Figure 9.1 Managing Change from the Outside In and the Inside Out (Source: CSC's Research Services)

	Outside In	Inside Out
	Define a sustainable business model for the supporting networked enterprise. ■ Use industry knowledge to define costs and benefits to participants. ■ Develop a fee structure to support sustainable growth. ■ Consider a nonprofit model where membership fees are used to fund projects that benefit the industry as a whole. Attract a critical mass of traders and collaborators to achieve liquidity. ■ Proceed only with support from big players for industry markets. ■ Include an advertising budget in the business plan for mass markets.	■ Develop a business case for collaboration. ■ Determine what kinds of partnerships are needed. ■ Identify and select appropriate partners.
	Define responsibilities and governance structures in the reworked enterprise. ■ Recruit major players (customers, competitors, and enablers) for your industry markets. ■ Define a clear commercial model for mass markets.	Develop externally oriented management roles and people to fill them. ■ Identify good career paths and senior management positions. ■ Recognize and reward business and IT managers who take externally oriented roles.
	Develop a dynamic organization that will define and manage cross-business processes. ■ Elicit ownership by and commitment from main players. ■ Develop the required business and technology modeling skills.	Recognize internal processes and management capabilities to support the cross-industry development of processes. ■ Identify the individuals with the skill and experience (gurus, coaches, and wizards) to interpret the wealth of information generated by the networked enterprise. ■ Give them leadership of efforts to define and refine cross-industry processes.

Figure 9.1   Managing Change from the Outside In and the Inside Out (continued)

	Outside In	Inside Out
		Create an integrated organizational model for the on-line channel. ■ Develop a detailed and comprehensive knowledge of internal processes. ■ Gain commitment from process owners. Promote collaboration between businesspeople, IT people, and external service providers.
	Define and manage cross-business collaborative projects (for example, process improvements, new products). ■ Encourage innovative ideas. ■ Demonstrate commitment to constant improvement. ■ Promote good project management.	Provide and support innovative experts. ■ Enhance your management's focus on knowledge as a key asset. ■ Gain the commitment to use it externally. Develop and implement partnership skills. ■ Develop shared understanding of different types of partnerships and how to choose and work with partners.
Technical Challenges	Build and run a networked enterprise. ■ Develop and deploy security procedures and technology. ■ Provide support for appropriate trading models (catalogue, auctions, etc.). ■ Provide support for coordination of routine processes. ■ Provide support for collaborative working (product data exchange, planning and design, etc.). ■ Provide for the capture and dissemination of cross-business information (trading volumes, process efficiency, etc.). ■ Provide support for value-added services (logistics planning, finance).	Update and integrate legacy systems to enable real-time processing. ■ Replace batch systems that will not readily support interoperability. ■ Deploy technology to support interoperability of internal systems. ■ Develop depth of experience in XML and JP. ■ Match your security procedures with your ambitions for a business. ■ Develop and deploy appropriate levels of security. ■ Explore emerging technologies such as BPMS.

Figure 9.1 Managing Change from the Outside In and the Inside Out (continued)

Outside In	Inside Out
Define a precise and comprehensive ontology for industry sector(s). ■ Obtain commitment from main players. ■ Assess existing cross-industry sources. ■ Recruit or train ontologists with deep industry knowledge and insight.	Create interfaces for flexible communication with a variety of tracking platforms. ■ Obtain management commitment to do it right. ■ Develop the ability of your staff to manage interdisciplinary teams. ■ Hire or train staff in architectural skills. Recruit expertise in use of XML.

Figure 9.1 Managing Change from the Outside In and the Inside Out (continued)

incomplete, and conflicting information; create new solutions; and find new ways to go to market. Provide them with the supportive environment they need to collaborative with each other and with customers and business partners.

Between businesses, this means using BPM to provide visibility and control of the flow of information, materials, and cash across application and business boundaries. It also means supporting creative collaboration, whether a simple chat room or a complex virtual R&D laboratory.

2. Do Only Those Things You Can Do at a World-Class Level and Find Partners for Everything Else

Your company needs to be on the front edge of just about everything it does for its customers today. This means that you must look at your business through your customer's eyes and invest in your strengths and divest the parts of the business that do not meet customer expectations. Plan to partner more and to partner in areas that are part of your core value proposition to your key customers. If some capability (safety, marketing, sales, or logistics) does not measure up, you may have the resources but are not likely to have the time to invest in upgrading the capability. More importantly, while you invest, your customers' needs may change. With BPM, it easier and faster to change partners than it is to build new capabilities.

Where you are world class, you have new assets to take to market. Your customers, other businesses, and even competitors are possible customers. All of this, however, is dependent on your ability to customize and manage business processes. Your business may soon be asked to display its business process models in operation. Due diligence may include inspection of your BPML libraries.

3. Align Through Standards, Not Applications or Hardware

Given the rate of change in your markets, your customers, your partners, and technology itself, you cannot expect to develop a standard technology platform for your own company, let alone dictate the technology your business partners or consumers will use. Even your employees are demanding the right to choose their own laptop, PDA, and/or mobile phone, and chances are they can get what they need at a lower cost than you are paying today! Therefore, use standards for security, message interchange, and process model definition to ensure interoperability.

4. Componentize and Then Use BPM to Take Control

Take advantage of the new wave of componentization sweeping the technology market. Microsoft and Sun are promoting componentization with their NetMarkets and Web services architectures. Large application vendors such as SAP, Siebel, and i2 are providing fine-grain access to the components of their applications. Carve your legacy systems at the natural joints. Then, use BPM to create the business process models that pull these components together to support your business processes in a way that gives your visibility and control across people, systems, and organizations. Use the power of the executable business process model to eliminate time-consuming and costly coding and to close the gap between the processes your business wants and the one your systems support.

5. Build Your Vision from the Top Down and Your Business Case from the Bottom Up

In today's climate of healthy skepticism, neither business nor IT executives are likely to believe that any new wave of technology is going to achieve significant business results without seeing the results of a successful project in their own business. This need not be a barrier to developing a vision of how BPM can transform the way your business can work with its customers and partners. It will, however, affect how to get started, how you build a business case for action, and how you build support for a wider program.

In our work on innovation, CSC's Research Services has identified three critical roles the CIO plays in building support for innovation. The first is creating awareness of the supply of innovative technology. For BPM, this would mean providing your executive team concrete examples of how this new technology could be used to achieve specific business goals such as faster claims processing, customized sourcing processes, and/or just-in-time manufacturing for specified customers. The next task is to make sure you understand the key areas of demand by working with your executive team to understand what your customers are asking of you. The final task is to connect supply and demand and to create a vision of a BPM-powered business.

The vision is not likely to win support or funding for implementing BPM. Although the funding you request will not be of the size and scale of former large change projects, you still must deal with skepticism from executives who have invested in past programs, from ERP to e-business, that have failed to deliver promised results. Also, your business plan will show a modest initial investment, but the total investment will be substantial.

The next step is simply to build support on a project-by-project basis, where each project must show significant return on investment. This will allow you to accumulate evidence in your business that BPM will provide return on investment. This bottom-up approach to business case design recognizes that executives are unlikely to accept a business case based on other businesses or industry benchmarks. BPM is too new a technology to have a credible track record. More importantly, too many investment decisions in the recent past were made on the basis of industry benchmarks that are no longer credible in light of recent exposures of questionable accounting practices at companies that provided many of the benchmarking numbers for e-business and ERP.

6. A Business Process Does Not Exist in a Vacuum

It is part of an interrelated business design that includes metrics, measurement, systems, culture, organization, and technology. A business process cannot operate without supporting metrics, measurement systems, culture, organization, and technology. A process that delivers radical improvements in business objectives inevitably requires changes to all five dimensions of the business diamond that supports the process, as described in Figure 9.2. Many projects fail because insufficient re-

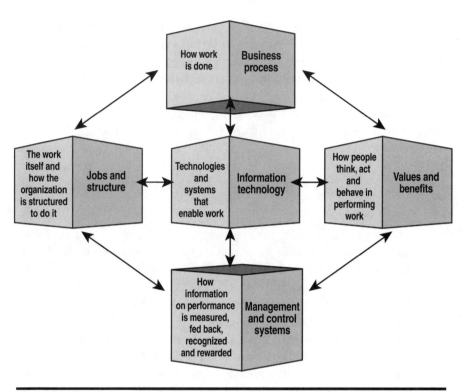

Figure 9.2   The Business Diamond of Values (Source: CSC's Research Services)

sources are allocated to make sure that needed changes take place in all five dimensions. A process is designed and systems are built, but many layers of management and line management staff use the old job structure and management systems to limit the scale of change.

Process design projects that cross business boundaries frequently ignore the need to align the businesses around all five points of the business diamond. Businesses with very different metrics, culture, and organization soon find that a common process is of little help in closing the gap between the businesses. The good news about this problem is that a proven solution is well known: a high-level executive sponsor who champions the process program and ensures that all five dimensions of the program are put in place.

That executive sponsor needs to be supported by a high-power, high-energy process owner who drives the day-to-day program to put the new business diamond in place. A similar remedy works in the multibusiness scenario. However, there needs to be an executive champion in each business, and these executive champions need to be aligned. The process owner then takes on the job of keeping the executive sponsors aligned, as well driving the change program.

7. Good Management Backed by a Virtuous Circle of Understanding, Targets, and Skill Sets Are Needed to Deliver Consistent Business Results

We have found that projects using innovative technology typically fail to deliver because of poor project management, not failure of the technology. Core project management skills such as the ability to set clear objectives for a project, recruit the right team, and manage management expectations become more, not less, important when using an innovative technology. As one CIO told us, you may outsource everything but key staff members who can speak to the business in business terms and are good project managers.

8. How You Implement a Process Improvement Program Is as Important as What Technologies You Choose to Support the Program

With almost every technology, we have seen different businesses use the same technology, sometimes with the assistance of the same consultants, with wildly different success rates. The apparent conundrum is explained by differences in mastery of the methodology needed to implement the technology and an understanding of the business and IT architecture needed to achieve the business goals. In all of our case studies, the business and vendor teams came to the project with proven business processes design methodologies that were rapidly adapted to the BPM technology. The focus was the end-to-end business process, not the technology. Many techniques (interviews, observations, and group sessions) were used to discover existing processes. The project team found discrepancies between what people actually did, what management believed the process was, and what management believed the process should be. These differences surfaced during the design and were resolved in the context of the metrics the process was to achieve for the customer as well as the business itself. In all cases, business metrics — not IT metrics — remained the critical success factors throughout the design and deployment process.

Business process design is not a one-time event. Customers, competitors, and change will reshape the market, creating the continual need to adjust, rethink, and replant. When creating a simulation center for process design, make sure that you allow time, space, and resources for continual review of process operations. Process teams need the ability to observe operations and to feed process operation information directly into the discovery and design process.

9. The Rhetoric of BPM Has Spread Faster Than the Reality

Thus the proof-of-concept projects are a good way to identify techniques that will work in your environment. The software, consulting, and systems integration markets have jumped on the BPM bandwagon. Vendors from many backgrounds are all delivering the message that they can solve today's business problems while leveraging your investment in older technology.

Usual methods of matching software choices to your business needs will help identify the relevant set of vendors. However, you will still be left with a set of relatively new vendors or with established vendors with new products and few references. The case studies have shown that the best way to verify vendors' claims is to invite them to do a "proof of concept" for your environment. In a few days they should be able to demonstrate that their solution will work in your environment. If the solution does not work in a few days, it is not likely to work with additional time.

10. Never Lose Sight of Critical Success Factor Number One: The Primary Objective of Process Management Is Improved Value as Perceived and Measured by Your Customers

Cost reduction is a good outcome but a poor objective. If you are not also achieving speed, quality, customer satisfaction, or some other outcome that provides value to your customers, you may be unwittingly committing to a strategy of competing solely on low price rather than value. Process improvement is not simply a cost-cutting exercise. You are eliminating low-value work and automating tasks to carve out time for your people to work with your partners to find new ways to create value for your customers.

Conclusions

In this chapter, we move closer to actual implementation, as we consider a ten-step process for execution. This effort gets started by choosing a BPM technology that provides the needed capability and proceeds to rebuild the business from the outside in. As skills are developed, the practitioners will learn that any helpful interenterprise project becomes a feasible endeavor.

10

FINANCIAL SERVICES COMPANIES ARE USING BPM TO LEVERAGE THEIR NETWORKS AND THEIR PEOPLE

Supply chain ideas are usually applied to industries like manufacturing and consumer products, which clearly fit the Michael Porter value chain model. The language of supply chain theory tends to assume a physical product, talking about solutions in terms of eliminating friction in the flow of information, cash, and product from the customer to the supplier. But almost every business could benefit from collaborating with partners, and advanced supply chain management (ASCM) ideas clearly address important issues for firms whose products and services are more abstract or digital in nature.

It could be argued that insurance, banking, and other financial services do not fit the Porter model at all, but the core issues of ASCM — optimizing value to the end customer and establishing visibility and control when partners work together to provide that value — are the same regardless of industry or business model. Certainly companies in this industry find that they have to manage complex processes that involve people, systems, and other business partners. When expressed this way, every business needs ASCM to distinguish it from competitors.

BPM Enables Financial Services to Leverage the Full Value of Digital Networks

From the outside, the financial services industry looks like the ultimate digital supply chain. Vast digital networks link suppliers, banks, shops, service providers, and customers. These backbone network services — the ATM networks, the digital financial markets, the check clearing-houses, and the funds transfer services — are automated and controlled by a few large-scale nucleus firms such as Visa and MasterCard, which specialize in commodity back-office processing. The long-predicted demise of cash has not happened, but the manual tasks, such as check processing, continue to decrease every year.

A closer look, however, reveals that these networks are used almost exclusively to automate simple transactions between firms, not as a platform for collaboration and ASCM. Financial services companies have used them to reduce transaction costs and to offer products and services with a global reach, but they often have only a limited view of their customers and very little ability to view a process as it winds its way through the value network.

What the customer sees as a result is a peculiar combination of inept service and a constant torrent of advertising and special offers. In *The Support Economy*, Shoshana Zuboff and James Maxmin (2002) document the way customer satisfaction has gone into free-fall despite all the costly customer relationship management (CRM) programs that have been implemented by financial services institutions. According to them, this chaos occurs because CRM has been used to harass the customer, committing, in the authors' words, endless "little murders." Call centers relentlessly push new services, product managers design irrelevant new products, and established firms find ways to charge new fees for old services. Customers are expected to conform to the way the company operates because companies seem to be incapable of developing processes that work for the customer.

This breakdown is usually blamed on the "culture" of the financial services industry. In general, the industry has been skeptical of process improvement programs, even resistant to them, because people-intensive activities are believed to be too complex and too sensitive to the context of the decision at hand to be documented and analyzed. Academics like John Seely Brown (Brown and Duguid, 2000) talk about the difference between process, which he defines as people or systems following a tightly defined script, and practice, which is a more fluid set of activities in which people react to each other in ways that are informed by skill and experience. Financial services are often asserted to be practice based rather than process based, and attempts to script behavior only result in mindless performance (which would obviously have a terrible effect on customer service!). Others claim that this is just an excuse for not trying — they are Luddites.

But in fact they have tried. There are huge known inefficiencies inside these businesses, between them and their partners, and between them and their customers, so they have repeatedly tried to automate processing — and they have consistently failed. But that is not because they are antitechnology or because their processes are too complex. The hidden barrier is the same one that has retarded progress in manufacturing businesses; so far, the prevailing technologies have simply not been up to the job. Technologies have been designed and deployed to automate processes completely and to replace people altogether. Such technologies are useless to businesses that need to help their people work more effectively by creating intimate mixes of process and practice.

For example, the U.S. home mortgage industry has always been very fragmented. The usual process map is illustrated in Figure 10.1. Digital networks link the market together, but there are pockets of manual processing within and between businesses, and each one is in effect an independent process. The customer, mortgage originator, lenders, aggregators, and secondary markets compete to maximize the value they can get from their position in the network. Each business also sets its own performance metrics — usually based on the speed of application processing and their individual return on investment. In the U.S. market, the end customer can easily get lost in such a confused network. At the end of the day, the firm servicing the mortgage is a distant, often nameless entity that simply collects payment — hardly the basis for a valuable relationship for either side. And when things go wrong, the customers typically take out their anger on whichever business they happen to be dealing with at the time. Unhappy customers switch lenders after a few years, leaving a bank with no way to achieve a return on its investment. The result is poor customer experiences, long cycle times, channel conflicts, and constant churn in the customer base.

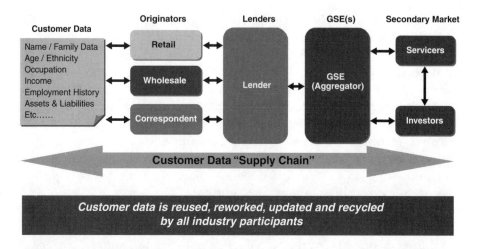

Figure 10.1   The Mortgage Industry: A Huge Customer Data Supply Chain (Source: CSC's Research Services)

In this chapter, we describe two examples of financial service firms that have successfully applied the new technology of business process management (BPM) and the principles of ASCM to their business. The first example is MetaBank, a major money center bank that has used BPM to manage some of its most complex processes. The result has been an annual saving of $3.5 million in a single process area. The second example is Norwich Union, which applied BPM to the people-intensive claims-processing area. In a matter of months, it managed to automate 95 percent of its claims processing and increased the efficiency of its claims-processing staff to the level of the best in the industry.

MetaBank Used BPM to Consolidate Processes and Find Savings

MetaBank is a world leader in securities trading. As one of the top five equity underwriters in the world, MetaBank trades over $2.5 trillion p.a. in securities, generating $7 billion or 40 percent of the firm's revenues.

In early 2001, MetaBank launched a major Six Sigma quality and cost reduction effort. While MetaBank was confident it could reduce its information technology (IT) costs by consolidating business processes and reducing its spend on infrastructure, it had no way of deciding which pieces it could eliminate or where in fact it might find bottlenecks that could slow critical business processes — costing the bank money, for example, when it missed regulatory deadlines.

MetaBank turned to its IT infrastructure provider, Computer Sciences Corporation (CSC), for a BPM approach to this problem. The challenge for CSC was to provide MetaBank with an end-to-end business process view of its IT applications and infrastructure.

CSC developed a three-step methodology process and tool set referred to as E^3M and iBPM to deploy BPM — business process modeling, integration, and monitoring:

- **Business process modeling**: The bank had done some business process work before, but process maps were not always up to date and they did not always provide sufficient detail. Using CSC's E^3M methodology, MetaBank defined its high-level processes from the business perspective and then mapped them to the participants (i.e., underlying support processes, applications, hardware, and network infrastructure) to provide a comprehensive view of everything involved. As shown in Figure 10.2, business processes had many hidden steps performed by IT systems or other businesses.

- **Business process integration**: Once the processes were mapped, BPM was used to integrate many systems used to monitor the performance of the underlying business applications and IT infrastructure. MetaBank could then track the state of each transaction while monitoring the performance of the business systems and infrastructure. The result was the ability to track processes end to end and the ability to track performance issues to the source of the problem. As shown in Figure 10.3, most processes were supported by a vast array of applications, infrastructure, and other businesses.

- **Business process monitoring**: Once the processes were mapped and integrated, the Intelligent Business Process Manager (iBPM) was deployed, enabling business users to view the state of the processes on Web-based displays. Displays include a stoplight chart that shows whether a process is running within established metrics and a spider web view that shows where and when it is not meeting goals. These views unify previously unrelated fault, health status, availability, and performance data from different

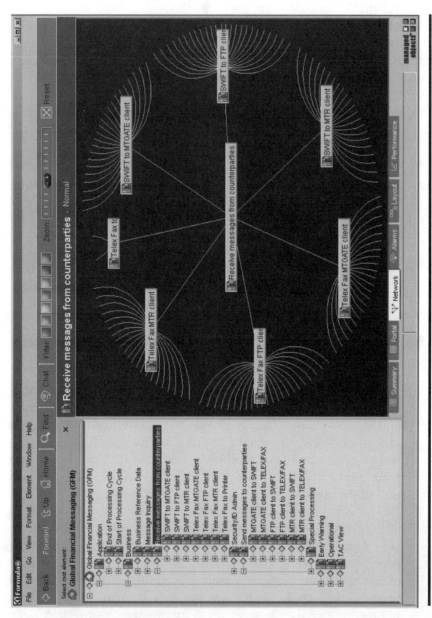

Figure 10.2 A Simple Process Has Many Hidden Steps (Source: CSC's Research Services)

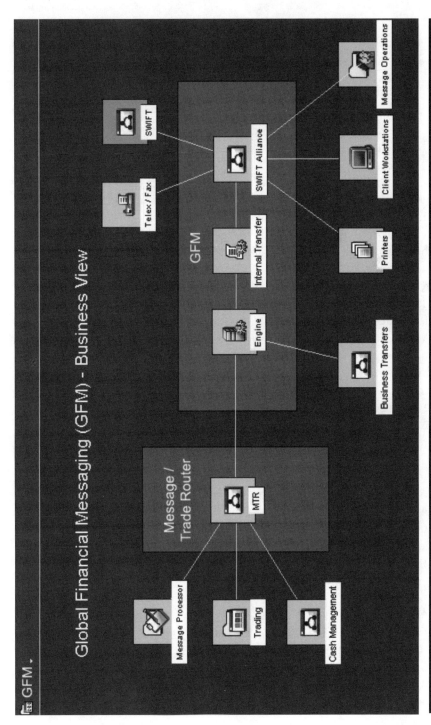

Figure 10.3   With BPM You Identify All the Participants (Source: CSC's Research Services)

underlying management systems and allow business and IT managers to view and manage the enterprise as a consistent structure of business processes, services, applications, databases, servers, networks, etc. Individual process owners are provided with the intelligence and control they need to prioritize problem resolution and optimize business service delivery. As shown in Figure 10.4, process performance could not be tracked using a simple dashboard.

CSC worked with MetaBank on a pilot project to develop an explicit view of the business processes of a back-end business support unit. This included the people who carried out critical tasks, the systems and IT infrastructure that supported the processes, and the other organizations, such as the clearinghouses, that played an important role in them. Armed with business process models that included not only people but also systems and other organizations, a BPM-based system was developed to track the contribution of systems from end to end and measure process performance.

MetaBank managers are able to see all the participants that support a business process and understand how specific business applications and infrastructure contribute to it. As a result, IT spending can be targeted on hardware, software, and infrastructure that are important to core processes.

Just as importantly, processes can be monitored in real time so that problems can be identified and resolved before sales are delayed or regulatory penalties are incurred. As a result, real-time measurement of the end-to-end processing is established, fewer penalties for missed deadlines are incurred, and trading transactions are closed faster.

A senior vice-president of MetaBank publicly acknowledged the contribution of iBPM to his business and the firm's efforts to improve operational excellence. A return-on-investment analysis of the iBPM implementation, from a third-party analysis firm, identified the annualized cost savings as approximately $3.5 million.

Norwich Union Used BPM to Demonstrate the Potential for Reducing the Time and Cost of Claims Processing

Norwich Union is the largest insurance group in the U.K. It has a reputation for innovation, such as the recently announced "Pay as You Drive"

Daily Problem Management Summary

Heat map

Investment Management | Global | March' 03 | Severity All | Show | Export

Service	1	2	3	4	5	6	7	8	9	10	11	12	13	14	15	16	17	18	19	20	21	22	23	24	25	26	27	28	29	30	31
Application			1	1	3		1																								
Data Restore			1	2		3	1																								
Desktop										1		1													1						
Facility																															
Hardware																															
Data Streams			2		1																										
Network			1			1																									
Printer																															
Purchasing																															
Security			1 2	2	1	1	1																								
Software			1	1		4	1																								
Voice			1																												

Severity = 1   Severity = 2   More details

Details of Service (Application)

CASEID	CDATE	PRI	COMPONENT	STATUS	CUSTNAME	LOCATION	DESCRIPTION
9402398	2003-03-03 10:49:48.0	1	CTG	Closed	Smith, John	Americas - NY	Trades-Processing application unable to process trades
9402411	2003-03-03 14:14:36.0	2	IMS	Closed	Doe, Jane	Asia Pacific	TView not working / layout has changed
9402425	2003-03-03 16:16:07.0	1	CTG	Closed	Jones, Sarah	EMEA - UK	Transactions not showing up in CTG. User unable to trade.

Figure 10.4 BPM Lets You Monitor Systems, People, and Organizations from a Process Perspective (Source: CSC's Research Services)

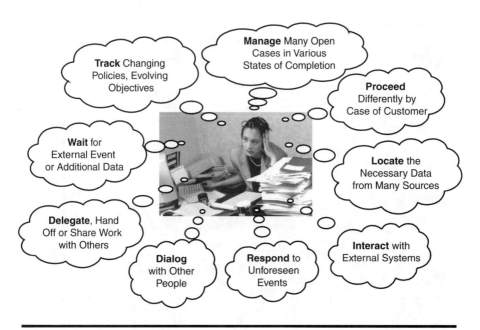

Figure 10.5   What Do People Do? (Source: Clear Technologies)

insurance scheme, where a vehicle is tracked by a built-in GPS system which is then interrogated once a month to create the bill.

In the aftermath of Norwich Union's merger with CGU in May 2000, senior management began looking for additional efficiencies in its heavily manual claims-processing function. At the end of the day, most insurance choices are based on price, so driving down the cost of claims is an important element of competitiveness. However, past efforts to develop applications to process claims had not been as successful as the company had wished. The claims-processing environment is very complex, and human beings perform a number of critical roles with a great deal of flexibility, as illustrated in Figure 10.5. Rules and regulations governing claims processing keep changing, requiring people to handle exceptions with costly manual work, which mostly consists of looking up legacy data, summing information abstracted from different systems, and applying the latest set of rules. Errors inevitably creep in and extensive rework is required. Norwich Union finally concluded that it needed a way to change its business processes that was faster than buying or writing new applications.

It decided to increase productivity and accuracy by using BPM to automate the routine activities, thereby allowing its claims workers to focus on the activities that really require their knowledge and experience. Fortunately, the company was aware of a start-up company that had been formed specifically to address back-office and case-file processing. Clear Technology's Tranzax product is a general-purpose BPM engine that automates long-duration, manually-intensive, and complex processes. In the case of insurance companies, Tranzax is used to address the problems of errors, rework, and delays and the difficulty in answering questions such as "Where is my claim?"

For test purposes, Clear Technology and Norwich Union selected the instances of claims against other insurance companies, partly because there were good baseline statistics about the existing process. The initial Tranzax solution was piloted with ten recovery handlers to evaluate it as a practical tool and make sure it would work in the Norwich Union environment. The strongly positive outcome of the pilot built confidence in the tool and the approach. Norwich Union is now developing the solution to roll out the project to 200 handlers. Initial results are positive, and it took just six months to develop the pilot mainframe interfaces, configure Tranzax, and perform all the layers of user training, acceptance testing, and production cutover in concert with the mainframe application release schedule.

The claims handlers themselves were pleased with the solution. Efficiency, accuracy, and staff morale are target benefits as the Tranzax product automates what were previously very manual activities, such as applying rules, tracking claims, and answering simple questions such as "Where is my claim?" The role of people is to make decisions, contact other companies, and follow up on collections. The claims processors have been enthusiastic about the new system because it takes the drudgery out of the work and helps them achieve targets for efficiency and accuracy. Their only concern is that they no longer need to leave themselves dozens of small notes to track cases. Their desktops are so clean that supervisors may think they are not working at all.

A significant learning point for Norwich Union was that conventional best-practice process development did not work for people-intensive processes. The conventional approach is based on the assumption that you have to get it right the first time because changing the process would take too long and cost too much. But this approach had never worked well in insurance processing for two reasons. First, business needs change more rapidly than the processes and systems that support them. Norwich Union itself introduces new products or services all the time and regulators impose new requirements on a regular basis. Modifying applications is too clumsy. Second, when activities are manual, there are no baseline process measures. It is hard to reengineer what you cannot analyze.

BPM makes change much easier because simply changing the process model can deploy a new process. This means that Norwich Union could deploy a baseline process based on observation of its most effective and efficient claims processor. In a matter of months, all the claims processors could be working at the level of the best performer, baseline measures can be established, and targets of opportunity can be established for reengineering the process.

This approach to process deployment caused tension with the IT staff, which had been used to a more traditional methodology of collecting requirements, specifying and designing a system, and then testing and deploying it. However, by demonstrating the business results of this new approach and by adapting release management methods to a much faster release schedule, Norwich Union was able to win IT support for the new way of deploying processes.

Norwich Union Intends to Apply BPM more Widely

The current pilot has shown that BPM can bring enormous improvements to complex, people-intensive processes. Norwich Union is now considering applying BPM to the processes within the claims arena and other areas. In taking responsibility for ensuring the repairs are done — and done correctly and cheaply — it has become the largest purchaser of auto parts in the U.K. It has become part of a classic supply chain (which is a new experience for a financial services company), and managing process complexity across multiple businesses is no longer a "nice to have"; it is Norwich Union's business.

Conclusions

BPM has demonstrated that technology can now be applied to people-intensive activities, where earlier technologies had consistently failed to bring any benefit.

ASCM is now every firm's problem. As companies compete on their ability to provide their customers with customized products and services, everyone has to be able to manage the complex and dynamic processes that they share with their supply chain partners. The new basis for competition will be the extent to which these firms' customer strategies take full advantage of the value network that results.

11

PUTTING BPM
TO WORK

In this chapter, we examine the experiences of three companies that have put business process management (BPM) technology to work in their supply chains. These are real firms that are going to level 4 of the supply chain evolution — and beyond — by integrating their processes with suppliers and customers and offering the ability to customize those processes as their partners require.

The first case is iUniverse, a new firm that has an innovative approach to publishing books. The second is LexisNexis™, a global leader in comprehensive and authoritative legal, news, and business information and tailored applications. Our third case is HiTechCo, a manufacturing company that wanted to improve the way it handled orders in its enterprise resource planning (ERP) system.

These companies have two things in common. The first is that none of them was actually looking for BPM technology; they just had a problem, and they were acutely aware that previous technologies would not solve it. The second is that they were all struggling to manage a complex situation and to be flexible at the same time. This is why conventional solutions would not work. Solutions that can handle complexity have not been good at handling change, and those that can handle change have only been adequate for handling simple problems.

iUniverse Is Reinventing the Publishing Business

iUniverse (www.iUniverse.com) was launched during the dot-com bubble, but it survives because it used the Internet to create a viable new business model. Funded by Warburg Pincus, a venture capital firm, and Barnes & Noble, a U.S.-based bookseller, iUniverse is using information technology to make it quicker, easier, and cheaper to publish books and to make the dream of being a published author available to everyone.

Through iUniverse, authors can get a book published and listed on the major catalogs within in a month, instead of the six to eight months that is more typical in the industry. Print-on-demand technology is used to fulfill small orders instantly — even in batches of one. Although the cost per copy is slightly higher than for conventional volume production, costs in other areas such as the setup for offset printing, large print runs, warehouse storage, and the pulping of unsold stock are all eliminated. This model provides a very cost-effective service to individual authors, but it can also be used by traditional publishers to reduce their risk in cases where they are unsure about printing a large run. The business model is complementary to traditional publishing, as opposed to in competition with it, as is often the case with print-on-demand services.

The Internet is important to the business model, not only as a way of communicating with authors but also because it means that iUniverse can be located anywhere and still deal with printers and catalogs across the world. In fact, copy input and revisions, along with the development and maintenance of IT systems, are currently done in China, while the rest of the organization is located in the United States.

iUniverse Faces Issues of Complexity and Change with Catalogs and Printers

iUniverse faces the dreaded combination of complexity and change in two key areas: in the way it connects to multiple catalogs to get books listed and in the way that it is connected to multiple printers to get hardcopy books produced in the right part of the world. Its initial approach was to throw programmers at the problem. It has good access to recent university graduates in China, so it can afford to have a lot of custom code written and changed frequently. Figure 11.1 shows how the company used custom code to take information from its database and transform it to meet the needs of particular catalogs. In the same way, it had

Pre BPMs Catalog Export Process(es)

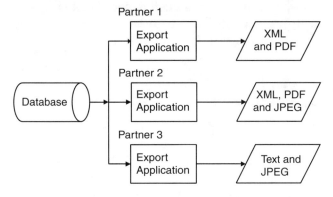

Other exports were handled as ad-hoc,
manual processes on a business
needs basis.

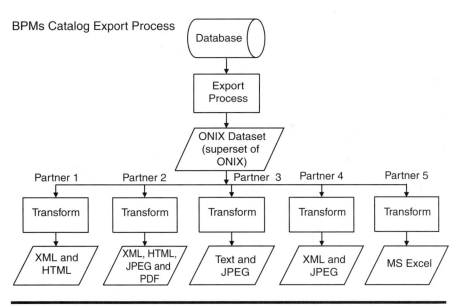

Figure 11.1   Conceptual Diagram of the Catalog Export Process (Source: iUniverse)

to produce electronic versions of books in formats that were acceptable
to each printer. Essentially, it had to hard code the solution for each
business partner.

iUniverse soon recognized that this was a very inefficient use of resources. It also saw that all this custom code made it very inflexible. It was difficult to implement changes because the engineering effort required was simply too great.

iUniverse Began Its BPM Implementation with Processes That Could Be Fully Automated

After internal discussions, Vernon Stinebaker, Vice President of China Technology and Operations, came to the conclusion that some kind of workflow or orchestration engine was needed that would allow iUniverse to compose business processes in a smart way. From this insight, the company developed a matrix of what it would need without committing itself to any particular product. The ability to reuse process components was the prime objective, along with visibility into the work queues. Recent positive experience with Java Messaging System (JMS) led iUniverse to include that technology as a "should have" ingredient as well.

With matrix in hand, iUniverse went technology shopping. It insisted that the vendor provide software for a practical evaluation because it wanted to know firsthand what it was like to build a solution and, because of the facility in China, thought it would be a good test of the vendor's support capabilities.

The company decided to test potential solutions on problems that would give a high return with relatively low risk and in an area that could be fully automated. For its first effort iUniverse chose to implement a catalog feed. Its catalog information is stored in a relational database and pushed out to partners in whatever way they want to receive it. Amazon.com, for example, uses the same catalog as Ingram but also wants a picture of the cover. The trouble is Amazon.com cannot receive the picture until after it has received the base information from Ingram.

iUniverse tried a number of different products, mostly with unsatisfactory results. In some cases, the product failed to perform even the sample test. In others, the product support was not up to scratch. The solution finally chosen was Intalio's Business Process Modeling Language (BPML)–based tool, n3. The Intalio solution had several advantages: it worked, it was stable, technical assistance was good, it supported a standard (BPML), and the Intalio concept of connectors made it easy to take advantage of JMS and not feel locked in.

Version 1.0 was not strong in its support of human interaction, but that was acceptable at the time because the initial focus was on full automation. With the release of Version 2.0 and the Director product, iUniverse was able to build Web screens and allow users to interact directly with the orchestration engine.

Figure 11.1 shows how the catalog export processes worked when Java code specific to each catalog had to be written and how this has changed since the BPM system has been installed. There is now a single process and the results are transformed for each partner using the XML technology XSLT. Managing variants and changes in this way is much easier than writing custom Java code.

Figure 11.2 shows an example screen from the catalog export process. The Intalio process design tool provides a visual environment in which activities and exchanges can be defined simply by dragging and dropping. The different participants in the process, which can be individuals, companies, programs, or other processes, are shown as vertical swim lanes. Once the flow between the participants is drawn, then each connection can be specified in more detail. A schema is dragged and dropped onto it to define the data to be passed, and it is given a connection "type," such as JMS, java beans, or SAP.

Figure 11.3 shows a fragment of the actual BPML for the catalog export process that emerges the visual process design tool. (Note that like most XML schemas, it is designed to be executed on a machine and is not really intended to be read by humans.)

The Main Lesson Is That BPM Works

One of the learning points from this project is that even if a product is easy to install and easy to use, there can still be significant learning involved in making full use of its capabilities. iUniverse strongly recommends investing enough time to learn to use the tool effectively. The visual environment is very powerful, but it represents a quite different way of solving business problems. Dragging and dropping is very different from writing procedural code, and even sophisticated programmers need some time to get used to this new way of working. Creating reusable code components also requires them to think of the business process in generic and abstract terms, which is quite a different mind-set from developing specific code for each partner.

The most important lesson iUniverse learned was that BPM technology did deliver on the promise. It does make it easier to handle both

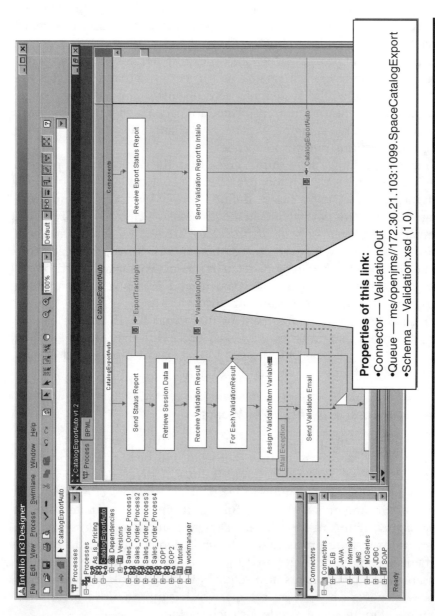

Figure 11.2 Intalio Designer Showing the New Catalog Export Process (Source: iUniverse and Intalio, Inc.)

```
<?xml version="1.0" encoding="UTF-8"?>
<package namespace="http://www.iuniverse.com" version="1.1" .
    xmlns:bpml="http://www.bpmi.org/BPML"
xmlns:rdfs="http://www.w3.org/2000/01/rdf-schema#">
    <process name="CatalogExportAuto.CatalogExportAuto">

...

        <message type="response" name="ValidationOut">
            <rdfs:label xml:space="preserve">ValidationOut</rdfs:label>
        </message>


...

        <consume idempotent="false" name="Validation">
                <input message="ValidationOut">
                    <assign target="ValidationOut" select="/*"
append="false"/>
                </input>
                <incoming
select="&apos;openjms://172.30.21.103:1099/SpaceCatalogExport&apos;"/>
                <session name="Starter_SESSION"/>
                <participant name="CatalogExportAuto.Components"/>
                <rdfs:label xml:space="preserve">Receive Validation
Result</rdfs:label>
        </consume>


...

    </process>
</package>
```

Figure 11.3   Actual BPML Generated by the Intalio Designer (Source: iUniverse and Intalio, Inc.)

complexity and change, not only for the tasks it was already doing but also for its larger aspiration of revolutionizing the publishing industry.

LexisNexis Wanted to Improve Its Handling of Orders from Small Law Customers

LexisNexis (www.lexis-nexis.com) offers an extensive range of on-line and print legal and regulatory information products, tools, customized Web applications, and critical filing services, mostly to large organizations. The company is famous for its wide array of information from more than 35,000 sources. Worldwide, it employs 13,000 people and serves customers in more than 100 countries. One of its key objectives is to increase the volume and speed of order handling for small law firm customers.

According to Terry Williams, Senior Product Manager, "Prior to implementing Intalio's BPM product such orders were faxed to Fulfillment and re-keyed from a faxed form into our Fulfillment systems. There were also manual checks being performed for business and licensing rules compliance. The process was time consuming and could be error prone. The end result could be delayed or incorrect customer orders and pricing and legal compliance issues."

The Potential for Greater Involvement of the Business Was Key to Its Choice of BPM

Independently, several groups within LexisNexis had been looking at ways of integrating the pieces of the order and fulfillment process. What caught the eye of the business units about the BPM approach was that they would be much more involved in the design of the system and, once done, they would be able to change it without having to involve the IT staff. More than anything else, it was the enthusiasm of the business units that drove BPM technology to the top of the list of integration contenders.

Fuego and Intalio were shortlisted, and both were presented with a list of 150 questions. Intalio was selected and started the program by integrating a field sales tool to send orders to a fulfillment area. The system automated clean orders completely but still allowed some manual input whenever it was necessary. Figure 11.4 shows the flow of the initial system.

Terry Williams is pleased with the results: "The order forms are now electronically submitted by the sales representatives. Intalio is being used to manage the business processes within Fulfillment. Business rules verification processes within Intalio are being used to alert Fulfillment of any compliance issues. The new process reduced the Fulfillment processing time for a typical customer order by 24 to 48 hours. We were also afforded the opportunity to reduce head count as a result of the Intalio implementation."

LexisNexis Will Extend Its Use of BPM

One of the helpful features of the BPM system is the way it holds data associated with the process as it progresses. Consistent data are carried

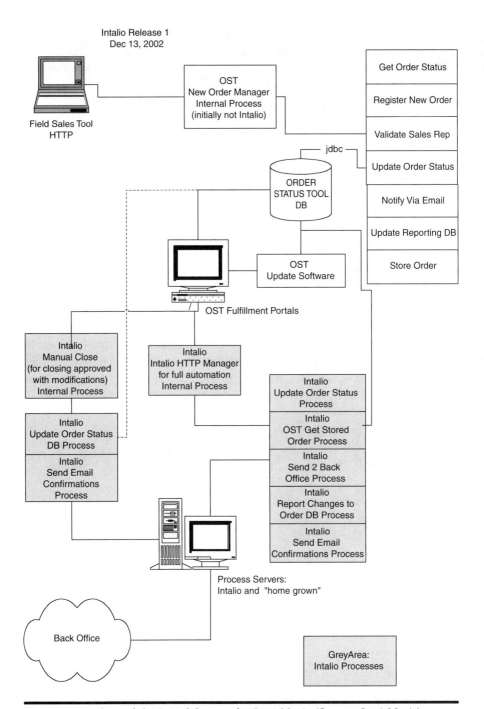

Figure 11.4 Flow of the Initial System for LexisNexis (Source: LexisNexis)

along with the executing process for all to see and use. The system also provided visibility of the time taken for each step of the process, which meant obvious areas for improvement could rapidly be pinpointed.

As with iUniverse, LexisNexis focused its initial BPM efforts on systems automation using its own Web tool for interactions with staff. With the advent of Intalio's Web interface tool, however, the company expects to extend its use into processes that have more human interaction. This will be especially important for handling special terms. If the state of Florida, for example, wants things done a little differently, LexisNexis will be able to create a special variant of the process. After that, when an order comes in from Florida, it can pop into a portal for review. This is all part of the drive to be able to handle exceptions easily and quickly.

The Lesson Is That It Works — But It Stretches the Brain

Like iUniverse, LexisNexis found the initial experience of building models in the Intalio visual design tool somewhat disturbing. As consulting software engineer Joe Pliss said, "I can feel a different part of my brain buzzing." BPM is a different way of doing things; it is a conceptual leap at least as big as when programmers went from mainframe Cobol to Object Oriented Programming on workstations. But it has brought a huge increase in capability. The LexisNexis back-end services can now be connected to any number of front ends in a relatively simple way. It's just a matter of getting up to speed with the new technology.

Pliss also emphasizes that it will transform the relationship between IT and other business units. He says it will be something like Extreme Programming, where two programmers work together on the same system. In Pliss's view, they may be on the verge of Extreme Business Programming, where a programmer and a businessperson work as a team to create a new business process.

HiTechCo Is Part of a Very Extensive Supply Chain

For HiTechCo, in the world of multinational manufacturing, it is obvious that no single company works by itself. The company is part of a very extensive, very complex, and very dynamic supply chain network. It does business with a wide range of customers and supplies a wide range of products, ranging from small, standard, relatively inexpensive parts all the way to large complex systems that might be significantly customized to meet particular customer requirements. Partnering and collaboration are essential if HiTechCo is going to deliver the right product to the right customer at the right time.

HiTechCo Wants to Adapt Its Order and Fulfillment Process to the Needs of Its Customers

One of HiTechCo's key corporate values is to be super pleasing, to both end customers and supply chain partners, to understand their needs and to exceed expectations. One part of the business that did not meet this goal was the order and fulfillment process. The main problem was that the ERP system that had been implemented would not allow the process to be adjusted to the needs of specific customers or to the characteristics of the particular products they were ordering. A secondary source of irritation was the way in which order errors were handled. As soon as the order process encountered an error of any kind, the order would be bounced back to the customer for correction — without checking to see if the rest of the order was okay. If an order had four errors, the customer might have to send it in five times before it would be accepted.

HiTechCo Did Not Want to Customize Its ERP System

HiTechCo faced a classic dilemma. It had a packaged software solution that did not do what the company needed. Who should make the change? And how? HiTechCo decided that to get it done right, it would have to take on the burden of making and supporting the change, but it wanted to do it in a way that minimized any extra work when the vendor released new versions of the ERP software. The thing it was determined to avoid was having to get inside the system and customize it.

The company concluded that BPM technology offered the right mix of flexibility and control and, after several rounds of competitive testing, selected Intalio's n3 solution. A key factor in the choice was Intalio's ability to "introspect" or to look inside the ERP system and identify the function calls and parameters it used. HiTechCo's ERP solution makes use of stored procedures that are located inside of an Oracle database, and details of these were uploaded into the Intalio design tool, making it easy for process designers to drag and drop them into new processes.

This meant that new processes, such as handling the error checking in a more customer friendly way, could be built into the Intalio tool while using the internal capabilities of the ERP system. As new versions of the ERP software become available, HiTechCo will simply introspect the new version, extract the details of the function calls and their parameters, and modify their connections accordingly.

HiTechCo Is Learning That BPM Attracts the Business — But That Means the Company Has to Communicate More

HiTechCo has not yet completed its development, but the lessons learned so far are unexpected and instructive. The first lesson came after a number of business staff were trained in the use of Intalio's visual process design tool and began to work with IT people on a particularly tricky process. The businesspeople were having some difficulty specifying exactly how a particular handoff should work, so, in an attempt to move things along, one of the third-party project managers suggested that they just get the highlights down in the diagram and let the IT people fill in the details later. This led one of the business representatives to say, "No! We are the ones who know how this should work, and we need to be the ones who specify it. You don't know how it should work, and that's because you were the ones to specify it in the past, and that's why we have crap for systems today!"

There would appear to be pent up frustration in the business because people have been unable to get their real needs embodied in the systems that support them. To some extent, this is because there has been no good way for them to express what they know in ways that could help the IT staff to execute. Drawing diagrams with tools such as Visio was not always helpful because there were no constraints on what was drawn. Activities could be represented with no inputs or outputs, for example, and the whole exercise lacked realism. Now it is possible to build the real system and to have both high involvement and realistic constraints on how processes operate. This appears to make for a much more engaging and productive dialogue.

The second important lesson that HiTechCo has learned is that the IT people become much more exposed to the realities of working in the business and introducing change — in other words, to politics. Everyone wants to close the gap between business intention and execution and to involve the business in the creation and change of systems, but the IT staff will have to develop some new political and communications skills.

It was a simple technical problem that brought this problem into focus because it turned into a significant political issue. HiTechCo made use of a product called Citrix, which allows PCs and other devices to act as thin clients to a server (which cuts down the cost of licensing and all the problems of updating software and backing up files). Intalio's visual design tool ran fine on it, but odd things started to happen, which made it appear that the data were being corrupted. The software was assumed to be full of bugs, and the rumor began to spread that the project would shortly be shut down and there would be egg on everyone's face.

It turned out that HiTechCo had configured Citrix to make everyone share the same user ID. This ensured that they would all use the most current software definitions, but it also meant that the users were constantly overwriting each other's profiles. For Intalio, it was a trivial matter to put in another level of user specification so that all the user profiles would be kept separate, but the rumor continued to circulate, unimpeded by facts. The usual technical review sessions that would normally have laid the issue to rest were not sufficient because the audience for this project was much broader than the technical community.

This new technology is very appealing for both business and technical reasons, but because of that it is extremely important to make sure that the business and technical communities are both kept up to date on the exact status of the project, what has been learned, and what issues, if any, are being worked on. In the future, HiTechCo expects to use a combination of passive (e.g., intranet sites) and active (live briefings of business staff) techniques to compete with the rumor mill.

Conclusions

Several important points stand out from these early BPM projects:

- BPM does make it possible to manage both change and complexity — and at attractive price points, making improved supply chain performance widely available and potentially changing the entire competitive landscape.
- BPM systems do make it possible for a business to get more directly involved in both the design and the execution of information systems. This idea has such strong appeal to business-people that it may become the overriding factor in choosing among technology solutions.

- BPM can help close the gap between technology and business-people by making processes explicit and measurable, but that means that IT will have to learn to operate in a new world where communication and politics are much more important.

12

BPM: CLOSING THE GAP BETWEEN BUSINESS INTENT AND EXECUTION

To summarize this book and to illustrate the potential of business process management (BPM), we present an article from a future edition of the fictitious business magazine *Fortuna Week*. In the article, the chief executive officer and chief information officer of logistics company ACME Express explain, from their different perspectives, how business process management systems (BPMS) technology has enabled them to escape the tyranny of legacy systems and regain control of their future business direction.

As you read the article, note that this is not about the distant future. This is a company that has chosen to be a leader, using BPM technology ultimately to develop a completely new business model, but everything described is perfectly possible right now. ACME Express could easily be a competitor of your business or, perhaps more likely, a supplier. It might be planning to ruin your business or to boost it; either way, it will be planning to take money out of your pocket!

Fortuna Week   **December 2005**

ACME Express Wins Logistics Innovation Award
for Business Process Management Program

The logistics industry has awarded this year's "Can't Believe They Did It"
award for innovation to ACME Express, the Wisconsin-based transport and
delivery company. Hilary Bloomberg, President and CEO, says that a major
part of the company's success was directly attributable to the new BPMS it
installed last year. Since then, managers have had unprecedented visibility of
what is going on in the business and the flow of improvement ideas has swelled
into a flood. But the really exciting thing is the speed with which the informa-
tion technology (IT) department has been able to implement these ideas. ACME
is rapidly becoming the market leader, she says, and the BPM program was the
turning point.

Fortuna Week: Can you explain for our readers what your BPM program is all about?

Bloomberg: It has completely changed the way we run our business.
The BPM systems are coordinating all our different business units and
feeding information back to me. I now have what amounts to a dashboard, which gives me up-to-the-minute information about what is happening in all our processes and compares it to our key performance
indicators. Better still, if one of my managers wants to suggest a change
in a business process, we can simulate the change and see the impact.
Sometimes, we demonstrate it to the board before we go ahead, but once
we've made a decision, we can implement things the next day.

Fortuna Week: So has it changed the way other people in ACME work?

Bloomberg: Absolutely! BPM has become a way of life for all of us. We
reorganized the entire business around our core processes and put all
the information about them in our process repository. That information
is now some of the most shared and the most reused in the entire
company. Our sales force uses it to negotiate deals, our operations folks
use it to find new efficiencies, our marketing department uses it in
simulations and what-if analyses, and our IT department uses it to negotiate contracts with service providers. Our legal and administrative
team has just started work on using it to protect our intellectual property
and get us qualified for ISO quality standards. You could say we have
uncovered a new form of business intelligence. It's empowered every-

one and stimulated completely new ways of planning and redesigning the way we work.

Another big benefit for me is that for the first time I feel really in control of the IT that runs the business — and I consider myself to be technology literate! IT always seemed like a "black art." I know it's vital to our future, but it seemed to be impossible to manage it effectively. What really surprised me was that the IT industry came up with the answer.

Fortuna Week: So how is BPM different from traditional solutions like enterprise resource planning (ERP) systems, knowledge management, workflow, and so on?

Bloomberg: They were at the heart of the trouble. We had all that stuff — and most of it worked okay in its own area, but we ended up with a lot of island solutions dotted all over the business. The bigger packages set up a kind of center of gravity and pulled all the stuff around them into their own way of working — what I call the Holy Grail effect — so we lost control of all these different bits of the business. We just had to go with the way the packages worked, and when we wanted to stitch them all together, oh boy! How deep are your pockets?

The beauty of BPM is that we don't have to replace all these applications. The BPM system can make them do what we want, and then it chains them all together into processes that we can see on the screen and change if we want to.

Fortuna Week: It sounds like magic!

Bloomberg: It felt like it, especially at first! It's kind of like glue that holds everything together, but glue with brains because we can use it to manage all the business rules, all the activities, and the events regardless of what technology is being used underneath.

Fortuna Week: A lot of CEOs will be skeptical; they still remember the last silver bullet. Isn't this just ERP on steroids?

Bloomberg: Not at all! ERP pulled a whole lot of stuff together when we first installed it, but it's still an island activity — just a much bigger one. It never connected easily to anything else, and I never felt like it put me in control. In fact, sometimes I felt like it was running me.

It was a solution to bad architecture. We did get rid of a whole mess of in-house solutions and all the tangled up connections between them and all the business rules embedded in them. And we got ourselves a real nice well-ordered closed system with all the business rules embedded in it instead. It also standardized things, which was useful in a lot of ways, but it came at a terrific cost. We had no way to differentiate ourselves around our core value propositions.

Fortuna Week: What's the difference between BPM and traditional business process reengineering?

Bloomberg: Hah! We tried business process reengineering in the early 1990s, but we pretty soon gave it up. Projects then were really one-time events. We came up with all these cool ideas and drew some huge charts, but we couldn't change much. I expect the charts are still in the cupboards where we left them. No one paid much attention to changes after that. I remember I came up with this way of handling orders better, but the IT people couldn't do it — not in the next two years anyway. In the end, we all lost heart in the effort.

But now BPM gives us a way of doing it easily, so you might say we are reengineering our processes all the time. We have some consultants to help, but everyone can understand what is going on, and we can do it all in small bites. We don't need big projects, like in the old days. We put stuff up on our intranet so everyone can see the changes from their perspective and how they'll help the business. People are getting really turned on to the whole thing.

What we used to have was all these bits of process buried inside all these islands — all these applications and packages — and we could never get in there to change anything and we could never join it all up. The real wake-up call was when our customers started asking us to join in their supply chain work. How were we ever going to connect up with them if we couldn't do it with our own systems? Luckily, the BPM idea came along just about that time.

Fortuna Week: So how does BPM help you to integrate with customers?

Bloomberg: And suppliers! Don't forget them. They were banging on the door, too.

Well, the secret is that BPM systems are designed to talk to each other. They're designed not to be islands. I have this picture of these two BPM systems and all the applications clustered round them, and then somebody puts them too close together and they rush together and join up. And then suddenly everything is talking to everything. Of course, it's not quite as easy as that — but not far off!

If the customer or supplier has a BPM system and it talks the same language, like Business Process Modeling Language (BPML), then we can build a model together and run the process between us. The systems handle all the messaging and handoffs, and we hardly have to think about it.

Fortuna Week: But how do you work out a whole process? And what happens if another customer wants something different? You can't do both, can you?

Bloomberg: Of course we can! We do. Why not?

Of course, we couldn't have done it in the old days. It was hard enough to work out one way of doing things, let alone two or three — or the eleven we think we now have. But the process model is just a script, just a piece of data, so we can have different versions for different partners and the system will make sure we do it right and make sure we always use the right one.

But even so, I thought the agreement problem would kill the whole thing. How would you agree on a whole process from end to end, even with one partner? Well, the trick is that you don't have to. All you need to do is to agree on a high-level shared model, what they call a public process, and then each side can have its own private processes so it can keep control of the bits that it does.

Fortuna Week: Doesn't that rather defeat the object?

Bloomberg: No. The main idea is to get things joined up. You could keep things secret, but that's not the main idea, and most of our partners don't do that. What happens is we all keep control of the details of what we do, so we can improve them if we want to. If we had to get agreement from everyone before we made a change, nothing would ever get done.

Fortuna Week: So must everyone have a BPMS?

Bloomberg: I can see a time soon when we'll expect our suppliers to be BPML compliant if they want to do business with us, but it's not that easy to dictate to customers.

Actually, we've done some interesting work with some of our big customers even though they don't have BPMS. It helped that we understood our own processes so well and had people who were really skilled in process modeling. We could get a handle on how the customer's process worked, which was usually in an ERP system, and then we could develop a customized logistics process designed especially to fit our needs. Then we could run this really smooth process without them having to change anything. They really liked that.

Fortuna Week: ACME has continued to expand globally. Has BPM done so as well?

Bloomberg: You can laugh, but in a way it has. The thing about a global logistics business is that it's all connected together. A parcel from India, for example, has to come via Europe and a couple of centers here in the U.S. before we deliver it, so we need to have the same processes all over the world. At the same time, things in India are different than in Europe and the U.S., so we have to give our people some space to do what makes sense in that environment. We have to strike a balance between global standards and local freedom to act — and that can be tricky.

As soon as we started to model our processes in the BPMS, the different countries realized that they could implement localized versions without sacrificing global interoperability. They found it extremely liberating, and they've been able to become much more agile in their markets. It stopped a lot of political infighting, too. It's more like horse-trading now. I say it would be a good idea to standardize this or that, and they can always think of something they'd like to customize.

We've been expanding through acquisition of local delivery firms as well, and BPM makes that a lot easier. We have models of all our processes, globally and locally, so it is easy to size up a new player and work out how they'd fit into our network. Then we can integrate them quickly more or less regardless of their IT legacy. That's not to say that BPM solves all the problems, but it does become a much more manageable process.

Fortuna Week: A recent publication described how you were creating BPM programs for supply chains and becoming a "Lead Logistics Provider." Could you expand on that?

Bloomberg: Yes, that was an idea that Barry Smith, our CIO, came up with, and it could be a huge opportunity for us. We decided to use our BPM experience as a launch pad for a whole new business model. We're going to move up the food chain and become a lead logistics provider (LLP), or what some people call a lead logistics partner.

We've proved the BPM concept in our core delivery business and started to model our partners' processes and integrate them. It's just a logical extension, to start providing a BPM service for a whole supply chain.

Needless to say, when overseeing and tracking an entire supply chain, everything has to work together totally seamlessly. But every supply chain works differently, so we have to look at each one as a BPM program in its own right. We act as an "infomediary," analyzing, orchestrating, and managing supply chain processes. We outsource the system implementation to a third-party BPMS hosting provider to demonstrate neutrality, and that means our IT folk can stay focused on our own BPM infrastructure.

We decided to leverage our experience in BPM as a platform for this business model. It's all about negotiation and trust, which is new territory for us, but we have a level of credibility, and the objective is to provide added value to all the participants in the whole supply chain. If it works the way we think it will, it could make more money than shifting their parcels around.

Barry Smith is the corporate CIO at ACME Express. He originally proposed the introduction of BPM and has been in charge of the implementation program ever since. Currently, he is working with Hilary Bloomberg on the move into the LLP space. He says that one of the most interesting changes this will bring is that IT will become a major money earner for the business.

Fortuna Week: Barry, could you summarize the key technical features of a BPMS.

Smith: There are a number of important pieces. First, there's the BPM engine, which connects to applications and coordinates the way they work. Then there's the process language, BPML, which is how we write the models, the scripts for the BPM engine to follow. There's even a query language, BPQL, for manipulating and interrogating the system.

Fortuna Week: How would you differentiate BPM from workflow solutions and, to some extent, collaboration tools?

Smith: Workflow and collaboration tools tend to be centered on human activity. They're an extra layer in the architecture, but pretty poorly integrated with the mission-critical IT applications. They can't provide the necessary continuity of real-world processes that span the entire business.

BPM is more like a completely different way of doing IT — and a different way of doing business comes with it. The program takes in human activity, applications, infrastructure, and business simulation and it allows us to implement completely new business concepts.

Fortuna Week: Models, repositories, and executable code. It sounds a lot like Integrated CASE. What's the difference?

Smith: Yes, I suppose it does a bit, but there are significant differences. BPML, the language, describes all aspects of the business and especially the way business-level transactions are executed. In fact, a BPM engine is more akin to a TP monitor than to traditional application. It maintains the state of business transactions as they are executed, whether it's by one of the underlying applications or by human activities. Its purpose is not to replace the applications but to support the higher level business purpose by orchestrating them and making them work together.

BPML is a kind of scripting language and not at all like application code. An obvious difference is the direct way in which we can execute changes to the processes. There is no concept of the traditional life cycle of requirement definition, application design, implementation, testing, and deployment. Instead of testing, we just simulate the impact of change before deployment and then changes are made "live" on the system.

Fortuna Week: How did you manage the transition to BPM?

Smith: Actually, BPMS support migration very well. You can model the behavior of an application — a so-called process projection — and then make that process a participant in another, bigger process. We found that the BPMS slotted right into the enterprise mix, and we were able to start deploying processes on it from day one. We started in one area of the business and implemented processes among the existing applications, and then over time we started to use the new system as a way of extending our processes to all parts of the business.

Fortuna Week: I presume that tool and package support for BPML is critical. Aren't you at the mercy of the software vendors?

Smith: I think that's a valid point, or at least it was. We first discovered the BPM approach back in 2000 through the Business Process Management Initiative (bpmi.org) when it had just started to gather momentum. In fact, we were among the first end-user organizations to join the BPMI. We had to satisfy ourselves that the concept would work, and we needed a critical mass of vendors working on the BPML standard before we risked embarking on a pilot of our own. It's true that in the early days we had problems finding software with native support for BPML, but in fact it's just an application of XML. We were able to work with our BPMS vendor to develop a range of BMPL adapters. But these days we are seeing a wide variety of vendors offering native BPML support within their products and services.

Fortuna Week: What's been the effect of BPM on the IT function?

Smith: It's had a bigger impact than we expected. We've stopped thinking of applications and packages as islands of logic and started using them as bundles of components, which can be used all across the business as a kind of infrastructure of services. The business thinks of itself more horizontally, and we're better at finding common application components that span functional and geographic boundaries.

We used to do a lot of business analysis within the IT department, but most of that is the responsibility of our chief knowledge officer nowadays. Previously, our corporate knowledge program was limited to human communication, and it tended to focus on improving collaboration independently of core processes. Now, we treat everything about our processes as knowledge, and my role as CIO is more focused on technology innovation and managing service levels.

We've been able to outsource some services, and because we now understand those processes much better, we have far greater control over the negotiation and the management of those services. And we've found that the service providers have benefited as well, because they get a much more explicit understanding of our needs.

From a technology innovation perspective, I found that although a lot of business analysis activities have been transferred to the knowledge management function, my staff is actually more motivated. I think it's because they can see how much value they're adding, and they're not constantly being blamed for failing to deliver. My sense is that we've finally found our place in the business.

Fortuna Week: So what do you see going forward?

Smith: I think the future is in being able to manage processes really well. We're becoming an LLP, managing processes across whole supply chains, and that means we must be world class, right on the leading edge of using BPM to make businesses work better — and especially to make them work better together.

We're experimenting with adapting processes in real time. There are a number of situations where the ability to implement "smart" processes that adapt to business needs would make sense. Our process models are held as data in our repository so they can be read and written by other software or integrated with other data sources, and we're working with new vendors in this area.

We've also found that because BPML is based on XML, we can easily extend it to add features that support adaptive processes. For example, we can take time and cost metrics and use them to adjust the switch points within the process based on thresholds or probabilities. For competitive reasons, we can't tell you what we're doing, but we can confirm that we intend to protect these innovative processes legally as far as we can, based on the BPML schemas and our demonstrable ability to execute them.

Fortuna Week: Fascinating. Thank you.

BIBLIOGRAPHY

Abramson, Eric, *Change Without Pain*, Harvard Business School, July–August 2000.

Bovet, David and Joseph Martha, *Value Nets Breaking the Supply Chain to Unlock Hidden Profits*, John Wiley & Sons, 2000.

Brown, John Seely and Paul Duguid, The Social Life of Information, *Sloan Management Review*, 2000.

Burlton, Roger T., *Business Process Management*, Sams Publishing, 2001.

Champy, James, *X-Engineering*, Warner Business Books, 2002.

Christensen, Clayton, *The Past and Future of Competitive Advantage*, Harvard Business School Press, Winter 2001, pp. 105–109.

Christensen, Clayton M. and Michael Overdorf, Meeting the Challenge of Disruptive Change, *Harvard Business Review*, March–April 2000.

Collins, James C. and Jerry I. Porras, *Built to Last*, St. Lucie Press, 1994.

CSC Research Services, IS at Work in Reengineering, Report 99, *Harvard Business Review*, 1997.

Davenport, Thomas, Business Process Reengineering: Its Past, Present and Possible Future, *Harvard Business Review*, 1995.

Davenport, Thomas H., *Mission Critical: Realizing the Promise of Enterprise Systems*, HarperCollins Publishers, 2000.

Dixon, J. Robb, Peter Arnold, Janelle Heineke, Jay S. Kim, and Paul Mulligan, *Business Process Reengineering: Improving in New Strategic Directions*, Harvard Business School Publishing 9-196-082, 1994.

Eisenhardt, Kathleen M. and D. Charles Galunic, Coevolving at Last, A Way to Make Synergies Work, *Harvard Business Review*, January–February 2000.

Fingar, Peter and Ronald Aronica, *The Death of "e" and the Birth of the Real New Economy*, Addison-Wesley Publishing, 2001.

Fingar, Peter, Harsha Kumar, and Tarum Sharma, *Enterprise E-Commerce*, CSC Research Services, 2000.

Hammer, Michael, *Beyond Reengineering Our Work and Our Lives*, HarperCollins Publishers, 1996.

Hammer, Michael, *The Agenda*, Crown Business Books, 2001.

Hammer, Michael and James Champy, Reengineering the Corporation: A Manifesto for Business Revolution, *Sloan Management Review*, 1993.

Hammer, Mike and Steven Stanton, How Process Enterprises Really Work, *MIT Sloane Management Review*, November–December 1999.

Handified, Robert B., Daniel R Krause, Thomas V. Scannell, and Robert M. Monczka, Avoid the Pitfalls of Supplier Development, *Sloan Management Review*, Winter 2000.

Imai, Masaaki and Brian Heymans, Gemba Kaisen, *Harvard Business Review*, 1999.

Jacobson, Ivar, Maria Ericsson, and Agneta Jacobson, *The Object Advantage: Business Process Reengineering with Object Technology*, Addison-Wesley Publishers, 1994.

Kasarda, John D. and Dennis A. Rondinelli, *Innovative Infrastructure for Agile Manufacturing*, CSC Research Services, Winter 1998.

Kontzer, Tony, Come Together, *Information Week Magazine*, October 7, 2002.

McCormack, Kevin and William Johnson, *Business Process Orientation: Gaining the e-Business Competitive Advantage*, Harvard Business School Publishing CMR 048, 2001.

Pawson, Richard, *Expressive Systems*, Berrett-Koehler Publishers, 2000.

Poirier, Charles C., *Advanced Supply Chain Management*, Berrett-Koehler Publishers, 1999.

Poirier, Charles C., *The Supply Chain Manager's Problem-Solver*, St. Lucie Press, 2002.

Poirier, Charles C. and Michael Bauer, *E-Supply Chain*, Berrett-Koehler Publishers, 2000.

Prahalad, C.K. and Gary Hamel, *The Core Competence of the Corporation*, Meghan-Kiffer Press, May–June 1990.

Slater, Robert, *The GE Way Fieldbook*, McGraw-Hill, 2000.

Slywotzky, Adrian J. and David J. Morrison with Karl Weber, How Digital Is Your Business? *Harvard Business Review*, 2000.

Smith, Howard and Peter Fingar, *Business Process Management: The Third Wave*, Meghan-Kiffer Press, 2002.

Sobek, Duward K. II, Allen C. Ward, and Jeffrey K. Liker, *Toyota's Principles of Set-Based Concurrent Engineering*, Wiley, Winter 1999.

Tempest, Nicole and Christian Kasper, CISCO Systems, Inc. Acquisition Integration for Manufacturing, *Harvard Business Review*, February 2000.

Tezuka, Hiroyuki, Success as the Source of Failure, *Harvard Business Review*, Winter 1997.

Thomke, Stefan, *Enlightened Experimentation: The New Imperative for Innovation*, Meghan-Kiffer Press, 2001.

Treacy, Michael and Fred Wiersema, *The Discipline of Market Leaders*, R.R. Donnelley, 1995.

van Der Aalst, Wil, Jorg Desel, and Andreas Oberweis (editors), *Business Process Management*, Springer, 2000.

Wetlaufer, Suzy, The Business Case Against Revolution, *Harvard Business Review*, February 2001.

Wise, Richard and Peter Baumgartner, *Go Downstream: The New Profit Imperative in Manufacturing*, Crown Business Books, 1999.

Womach, James P. and Daniel T. Jones, Beyond Toyota: How to Root Out Waste and Pursue Perfection, *Harvard Business Review*, September 1996.

Zuboff, Shoshana and James Maxmin, *The Support Economy*, Viking, 2002.

INDEX